CW01522421

Hamlet
Annotation-Friendly Edition

William Shakespeare

This book is also available in large-print, extra large print and dyslexia-friendly editions

firestonebooks.com

Hamlet
Annotation-Friendly Edition

William Shakespeare

2019 Edition

Published by Firestone Books

ISBN-13: 9781796716856

firestonebooks.com

You can also find out more by following Firestone Books on Facebook and Twitter

CONTENTS

`

A Quick Guide to Successful Annotating

- Write down any thoughts you have as you go along
- Highlight key points, either with a highlighter or by underlining
- Note any literary techniques in the margins. (The *Glossary of Literary Terms* at the back of the book should help)
- Define any words you don't understand – it will help you later
- Look for patterns, such as repeating words and phrases
- Pick out key points that show a character's development
- Summarise your thoughts on the blank pages at the end of each act
- Once you've finished reading the play, go back and add to your notes. In particular look at foreshadowing, echoing and motifs

William Shakespeare – A Brief Biography

William Shakespeare was born in Stratford-upon-Avon, the son of John Shakespeare, a successful glove-maker, and Mary Arden, the daughter of a prosperous farmer. His date of birth is unknown but he was baptised, most likely within a few days of his birth, on 26th April 1564.

It is likely that Shakespeare attended the King's New School in Stratford-upon-Avon where he would have received a classical education. He did not attend university, and at the age of eighteen he married Anne Hathaway who was eight years his senior. Six months later, in May 1583, Anne gave birth to a daughter, Susanna. In 1585 Anne also gave birth to twins, Hamnet and Judith.

Between 1585 and 1592 almost nothing is known of Shakespeare's life, the so called "lost years". Many apocryphal tales about this period have been reported including that he fled his hometown for London to escape prosecution for deer poaching, that he started his theatrical career minding the horses of wealthy theatregoers, and that he may have been briefly employed as a schoolmaster in Lancashire.

By 1592 Shakespeare was an established playwright, with several of his plays having been staged in London. It is also the year that fellow playwright, Robert Greene, published his infamous *Groats-Worth of Wit* in which he attacked Shakespeare for trying to match the writing of university educated writers such as Christopher Marlowe and Thomas Nashe.

Shakespeare's plays were only performed by the Lord Chamberlain's Men, a company of actors, in which Shakespeare had a share.

In 1596, Shakespeare's only son, Hamnet, died, and

while in later years Shakespeare's daughters would marry and have four children between them, none of Shakespeare's grandchildren would have children of their own, and so in 1670 with the death of his granddaughter, Elizabeth, his direct line was ended.

In 1599 some members of the Lord Chamberlain's Men built their own theatre on the south bank of the river Thames and named it the Globe. As a shareholder in this theatre, holding up to 3000 spectators, Shakespeare became a wealthy man.

Prior to 1599 Shakespeare had only written two tragedies: *Titus Andronicus* and *Romeo and Juliet*, with his focus being more on comedies, history plays and poems. After 1599 he almost stopped writing history plays and instead switched to writing tragedies, writing many of his finest plays including: *Hamlet, Othello, King Lear* and *Macbeth*.

In 1603 the new king, James I, awarded the Lord Chamberlain's Men a royal patent and the company changed its name to the King's Men.

As well as writing plays, Shakespeare also wrote two long poems and a collection of sonnets. The sonnets describe two love affairs, but who these lovers were – or even if they were real or imagined – remains a mystery.

As Shakespeare was also an actor, it meant that rather than working on his plays in isolation he would have worked closely with other actors. Many of the plots for the plays came from history books, or earlier Italian tales, so it is difficult, if not impossible, to work out what contributions were Shakespeare's. Even when he'd finished a particular play, it was still likely to be re-worked by actors and others – something that is done to this day and keeps his work as fresh and interesting as its ever been.

Though Shakespeare worked as a writer and actor

in London for most of his adult life, his did spend much of his time in Stratford-upon-Avon where, in 1597, he bought New Place as his family home. It's known that Shakespeare was still working as an actor in London in 1608, and that he also retired to Stratford 'some years before his death'.

Shakespeare died on the 23rd of April 1616, around the time of his 52nd birthday. It was said by John Ward, the vicar of Stratford, writing in the mid-1600s that 'Shakespeare, Drayton and Ben Johnson had a merry meeting and, it seems, drank too hard, for Shakespeare died of a fever there contracted.'

Shakespeare was buried at the Holy Trinity Church, the place of his baptism over half a century earlier. The epitaph on his gravestone has a curse against disturbing his resting place:

> *Good friend, for Jesus' sake forbear,*
> *To dig the dust enclosed here.*
> *Blessed be the man that spares these stones,*
> *And cursed be he that moves my bones.*

Fellow dramatist, Ben Johnson, famously and presciently referred to Shakespeare as being 'not of an age, but for all time.' Since his death Shakespeare's reputation has grown, leading him to now be widely regarded as the greatest writer in the English language and the world's greatest dramatist.

Introduction

William Shakespeare is the most-admired, certainly the most well-known now, of playwrights from a crucial period in the history of English drama. *Hamlet,* written at the very end of the sixteenth century, is Shakespeare's longest and most-quoted play. As the full title *Hamlet, Prince of Denmark* hints, the play is set in Denmark, mainly at a place referred to as Elsinore Castle. Kronborg Castle on the outskirts of Elsinore, north of Copenhagen, was the home of the Danish royal family until the late seventeenth century and now hosts open air productions of *Hamlet* every summer.

You may wonder what made William Shakespeare, a man from Warwickshire, write a play about the Danish royal family. The short answer is that he didn't, he rewrote someone else's play for his own company of actors to perform. We are used to original ideas in literature, after all the word 'novel' means new and unusual, as well as a long work of fiction. However, in Shakespeare's time there was no similar expectation and the idea of retelling older stories has never completely gone away, indeed many films and plays are adapted from short stories or novels today.

It's worth remembering that Shakespeare was an actor before he was a playwright so he was familiar with and may have acted in many plays that he later borrowed elements from. We know there was another play about Hamlet and a ghost being performed in late sixteenth century England, because people of the time mention it. However, the text of that play has not survived. Ultimately it was based on a story in a history of Denmark written around 1200 by a man known as Saxo Grammaticus.

Hamlet is famous for its soliloquies – the parts of the play where a character talks to themselves, allowing the audience a glimpse into what's going on in their mind. However, like the plot itself, the use of soliloquies isn't original. Soliloquies are a feature of *Spanish Tragedy* by Thomas Kyd, for instance, another popular revenge tragedy first performed in 1587. *Hamlet* then provided inspiration in turn, as Thomas Middleton opened his 1606 play *The Revenger's Tragedy* with a scene where a character holds a skull as he speaks, as Hamlet holds the skull of Yorick.

Revenge tragedies were popular in the late sixteenth century but unlike Shakespeare's earlier, gory revenge story *Titus Andronicus*, *Hamlet* is not that straightforward. Despite being directly asked by the ghost of his father to exact revenge, Hamlet hesitates, he pauses to reflect on the truth and the ethics of the situation. The complexity of the character is shown through this indecision. Importantly, Hamlet is portrayed as a student, which reflects sixteenth century ideas of educating a prince – he should be intellectual and have a grounding in the classics, rather than simply being brought up to be a skilled horseman and fighter as a medieval prince would have been.

Hamlet is a notably long play, which is not surprising given how complex it is, involving several major plot lines. There is family drama, love, revenge, murder, suicide, and a play within the play. It is a truly powerful work, addressing a number of ethical questions. The title role of Hamlet has come to be seen as the defining role for a serious actor because of its complexity and subtlety.

"To be or not to be, that is the question" is possibly the most famous line in the play but interestingly it does not appear in that form in the earliest printed version of the play we know, nor is it at the point in the play we're used to it being spoken. This is a good reminder that *Hamlet* was written to be performed and thus liable to be rewritten depending on what worked on the stage.

That also means the language is meant to be spoken with feeling, not skim-read on a page, and just as song lyrics feel a bit flat when they're written down, you don't get the full effect by reading the play as if it were a novel. Read it aloud or, if that's too embarrassing, find someone reading it aloud online and listen to them as you read along. Shakespeare deliberately switched between verse and prose for instance, to create a contrast or a change of mood, and these are easily lost when you simply look at the words.

Punning was popular in Elizabethan times, so as with many of Shakespeare's plays there are plays on words and a revelling in the flexibility of the English language. This flexibility extends to coining new words and phrases, many of which we use today, such as "Neither a borrower nor a lender be", "to thine own self be true", or in a slightly altered form rather than as a direct quote, "Though this be madness, yet there is method in it" (we might say "There's method in my madness").

There are countless references to *Hamlet* in popular culture, from comedy sketches to adverts, that assume everyone knows enough about the play to get the reference. Tom Stoppard's famous nineteen-sixties play *Rosencrantz and Guildenstern Are Dead* centres on two minor characters from *Hamlet* and uses wordplay to great effect. Characters from *Hamlet* also appear in Jasper Fforde's Thursday Next comic fantasy series, particularly the fourth novel *Something Rotten,* the title of which is of course a reference to the line "Something is rotten in the state of Denmark".

Many famous writers have written about the play, it has been discussed again and again for the last few hundred years, but there is so much contained within it that people will return to *Hamlet* for many years to come.

Jacqueline Saville
writer and reviewer

HAMLET

Dramatis Personae

Claudius, King of Denmark

Hamlet, son to the former, and nephew to the present King

Polonius, Lord Chamberlain

Horatio, friend to Hamlet

Laertes, son to Polonius

Voltemand, Ambassador to Norway

Cornelius, Ambassador to Norway

Rosencrantz, courtier

Guildenstern, courtier

Osric, courtier

A Gentleman

A Priest

Marcellus, officer

Bernardo, officer

Francisco, a soldier

Reynaldo, servant to Polonius

Players. two Clowns, gravediggers

Fortinbras, Prince of Norway

A Norwegian Captain

English Ambassadors

Getrude, Queen of Denmark, mother to Hamlet

Ophelia, daughter to Polonius

Lords, Ladies, Officers, Soldiers, Sailors,
Messengers and Attendants

Ghost of Hamlet's Father

ACT I

Scene I - Elsinore. A platform before the Castle.

[Francisco, at his post. Bernardo approaches him.]

Bernardo: Who's there?

Francisco: Nay, answer me. Stand and unfold yourself.

Bernardo: Long live the King!

Francisco: Bernardo?

Bernardo: He.

Francisco: You come most carefully upon your hour.

Bernardo: 'Tis now struck twelve. Get thee to bed, Francisco.

Francisco: For this relief much thanks. 'Tis bitter cold,

And I am sick at heart.

Bernardo: Have you had quiet guard?

Francisco: Not a mouse stirring.

Bernardo: Well, good night.

If you do meet Horatio and Marcellus,

The rivals of my watch, bid them make haste.

[Enter Horatio and Marcellus.]

Francisco: I think I hear them. Stand, ho! Who is there?

Horatio: Friends to this ground.

Marcellus: And liegemen to the Dane.

Francisco: Give you good night.

Marcellus: O, farewell, honest soldier.

Who hath reliev'd you?

Francisco: Bernardo hath my place.

Give you good night.

[Exit.]

Marcellus: Holla, Bernardo!

Bernardo: Say-

What, is Horatio there ?

Horatio: A piece of him.

Bernardo: Welcome, Horatio. Welcome, good Marcellus.

Marcellus: What, has this thing appear'd again to-night?

Bernardo: I have seen nothing.

Marcellus: Horatio says 'tis but our fantasy,

And will not let belief take hold of him

Touching this dreaded sight, twice seen of us.

Therefore I have entreated him along,

With us to watch the minutes of this night,

That, if again this apparition come,

He may approve our eyes and speak to it.

Horatio: Tush, tush, 'twill not appear.

Bernardo: Sit down awhile,

And let us once again assail your ears,

That are so fortified against our story,

What we two nights have seen.

Horatio: Well, sit we down,

And let us hear Bernardo speak of this.

Bernardo: Last night of all,

When yond same star that's westward from the pole

Had made his course to illume that part of heaven

Where now it burns, Marcellus and myself,

The bell then beating one-

[Enter Ghost.]

Marcellus: Peace! break thee off! Look where it comes again!

Bernardo: In the same figure, like the King that's dead.

Marcellus: Thou art a scholar; speak to it,

Horatio.

Bernardo: Looks it not like the King? Mark it, Horatio.

Horatio: Most like. It harrows me with fear and wonder.

Bernardo: It would be spoke to.

Marcellus: Question it, Horatio.

Horatio: What art thou that usurp'st this time of night

Together with that fair and warlike form

In which the majesty of buried Denmark

Did sometimes march? By heaven I charge thee speak!

Marcellus: It is offended.

Bernardo: See, it stalks away!

Horatio: Stay! Speak, speak! I charge thee speak!

[Exit Ghost.]

Marcellus: 'Tis gone and will not answer.

Bernardo: How now, Horatio? You tremble and look pale.

Is not this something more than fantasy?

What think you on't?

Horatio: Before my God, I might not this believe

Without the sensible and true avouch

Of mine own eyes.

Marcellus: Is it not like the King?

Horatio: As thou art to thyself.

Such was the very armour he had on

When he th' ambitious Norway combated.

So frown'd he once when, in an angry parle,

He smote the sledded Polacks on the ice.

'Tis strange.

Marcellus: Thus twice before, and jump at this dead hour,

With martial stalk hath he gone by our watch.

Horatio: In what particular thought to work I know not;

But, in the gross and scope of my opinion,

This bodes some strange eruption to our state.

Marcellus: Good now, sit down, and tell me he that knows,

Why this same strict and most observant watch

So nightly toils the subject of the land,

And why such daily cast of brazen cannon

And foreign mart for implements of war;

Why such impress of shipwrights, whose sore task

Does not divide the Sunday from the week.

What might be toward, that this sweaty haste

Doth make the night joint-labourer with the day?

Who is't that can inform me?

Horatio: That can I.

At least, the whisper goes so. Our last king,

Whose image even but now appear'd to us,

Was, as you know, by Fortinbras of Norway,

Thereto prick'd on by a most emulate pride,

Dar'd to the combat; in which our valiant Hamlet

 (For so this side of our known world esteem'd him)

Did slay this Fortinbras; who, by a seal'd compact,

Well ratified by law and heraldry,

Did forfeit, with his life, all those his lands

Which he stood seiz'd of, to the conqueror;

Against the which a moiety competent

Was gaged by our king; which had return'd

To the inheritance of Fortinbras,

Had he been vanquisher, as, by the same co-mart

And carriage of the article design'd,

His fell to Hamlet. Now, sir, young Fortinbras,

Of unimproved mettle hot and full,

Hath in the skirts of Norway, here and there,

Shark'd up a list of lawless resolutes,

For food and diet, to some enterprise

That hath a stomach in't; which is no other,

As it doth well appear unto our state,

But to recover of us, by strong hand

And terms compulsatory, those foresaid lands

So by his father lost; and this, I take it,

Is the main motive of our preparations,

The source of this our watch, and the chief head

Of this post-haste and romage in the land.

Bernardo: I think it be no other but e'en so.

Well may it sort that this portentous figure

Comes armed through our watch, so like the King

That was and is the question of these wars.

Horatio: A mote it is to trouble the mind's eye.

In the most high and palmy state of Rome,

A little ere the mightiest Julius fell,

The graves stood tenantless, and the sheeted dead

Did squeak and gibber in the Roman streets;

As stars with trains of fire, and dews of blood,

Disasters in the sun; and the moist star

Upon whose influence Neptune's empire stands

Was sick almost to doomsday with eclipse.

And even the like precurse of fierce events,

As harbingers preceding still the fates

And prologue to the omen coming on,

Have heaven and earth together demonstrated

Unto our climature and countrymen.

[Enter Ghost again.]

But soft! behold! Lo, where it comes again!

I'll cross it, though it blast me. Stay illusion!

[Spreads his arms.]

If thou hast any sound, or use of voice,

Speak to me.

If there be any good thing to be done,

That may to thee do ease, and, race to me,

Speak to me.

If thou art privy to thy country's fate,

Which happily foreknowing may avoid,

O, speak!

Or if thou hast uphoarded in thy life

Extorted treasure in the womb of earth

(For which, they say, you spirits oft walk in

death),

[The cock crows.]

Speak of it! Stay, and speak!- Stop it, Marcellus!

Marcellus: Shall I strike at it with my partisan?

Horatio: Do, if it will not stand.

Bernardo: 'Tis here!

Horatio: 'Tis here!

Marcellus: 'Tis gone!

[Exit Ghost.]

We do it wrong, being so majestical,

To offer it the show of violence;

For it is as the air, invulnerable,

And our vain blows malicious mockery.

Bernardo: It was about to speak, when the cock

crew.

Horatio: And then it started, like a guilty thing

Upon a fearful summons. I have heard

The cock, that is the trumpet to the morn,

Doth with his lofty and shrill-sounding throat

Awake the god of day; and at his warning,

Whether in sea or fire, in earth or air,

Th' extravagant and erring spirit hies

To his confine; and of the truth herein

This present object made probation.

Marcellus: It faded on the crowing of the cock.

Some say that ever, 'gainst that season comes
Wherein our Saviour's birth is celebrated,
The bird of dawning singeth all night long;
And then, they say, no spirit dare stir abroad,
The nights are wholesome, then no planets
strike,
No fairy takes, nor witch hath power to charm,
So hallow'd and so gracious is the time.
Horatio: So have I heard and do in part believe
it.
But look, the morn, in russet mantle clad,
Walks o'er the dew of yon high eastward hill.
Break we our watch up; and by my advice
Let us impart what we have seen to-night
Unto young Hamlet; for, upon my life,
This spirit, dumb to us, will speak to him.
Do you consent we shall acquaint him with it,
As needful in our loves, fitting our duty?
Let's do't, I pray; and I this morning know
Where we shall find him most conveniently.
[Exeunt.]

Scene II - Elsinore. The Council Chamber in the Castle.

[Flourish. Enter Claudius, King of Denmark, Gertrude the Queen, Hamlet, Polonius, Laertes, Ophelia, Voltemand, Cornelius, Lords and Attendant.]

King: Though yet of Hamlet our dear brother's death
The memory be green, and that it us befitted
To bear our hearts in grief, and our whole kingdom
To be contracted in one brow of woe,
Yet so far hath discretion fought with nature
That we with wisest sorrow think on him
Together with remembrance of ourselves.
Therefore our sometime sister, now our queen,
Th' imperial jointress to this warlike state,
Have we, as 'twere with a defeated joy,
With an auspicious, and a dropping eye,
With mirth in funeral, and with dirge in marriage,
In equal scale weighing delight and dole,
Taken to wife; nor have we herein barr'd
Your better wisdoms, which have freely gone

With this affair along. For all, our thanks.
Now follows, that you know, young Fortinbras,
Holding a weak supposal of our worth,
Or thinking by our late dear brother's death
Our state to be disjoint and out of frame,
Colleagued with this dream of his advantage,
He hath not fail'd to pester us with message
Importing the surrender of those lands
Lost by his father, with all bands of law,
To our most valiant brother. So much for him.
Now for ourself and for this time of meeting.
Thus much the business is: we have here writ
To Norway, uncle of young Fortinbras,
Who, impotent and bedrid, scarcely hears
Of this his nephew's purpose, to suppress
His further gait herein, in that the levies,
The lists, and full proportions are all made
Out of his subject; and we here dispatch
You, good Cornelius, and you, Voltemand,
For bearers of this greeting to old Norway,
Giving to you no further personal power
To business with the King, more than the scope
Of these dilated articles allow. [Gives a paper.]
Farewell, and let your haste commend your duty.

Cornelius and Voltemand: In that, and all things, will we show our duty.

King: We doubt it nothing. Heartily farewell.

[Exeunt Voltemand and Cornelius.]

And now, Laertes, what's the news with you?

You told us of some suit. What is't, Laertes?

You cannot speak of reason to the Dane

And lose your voice. What wouldst thou beg, Laertes,

That shall not be my offer, not thy asking?

The head is not more native to the heart,

The hand more instrumental to the mouth,

Than is the throne of Denmark to thy father.

What wouldst thou have, Laertes?

Laertes: My dread lord,

Your leave and favour to return to France;

From whence though willingly I came to Denmark

To show my duty in your coronation,

Yet now I must confess, that duty done,

My thoughts and wishes bend again toward France

And bow them to your gracious leave and pardon.

King: Have you your father's leave? What says Polonius?

Polonius: He hath, my lord, wrung from me my slow leave

By laboursome petition, and at last

Upon his will I seal'd my hard consent.

I do beseech you give him leave to go.

King: Take thy fair hour, Laertes. Time be thine,

And thy best graces spend it at thy will!

But now, my cousin Hamlet, and my son-

Hamlet: [aside] A little more than kin, and less than kind!

King: How is it that the clouds still hang on you?

Hamlet: Not so, my lord. I am too much i' th' sun.

Queen: Good Hamlet, cast thy nighted colour off,

And let thine eye look like a friend on Denmark.

Do not for ever with thy vailed lids

Seek for thy noble father in the dust.

Thou know'st 'tis common. All that lives must die,

Passing through nature to eternity.

Hamlet: Ay, madam, it is common.

Queen: If it be,

Why seems it so particular with thee?

Hamlet: Seems, madam, Nay, it is. I know not

'seems.'

'Tis not alone my inky cloak, good mother,

Nor customary suits of solemn black,

Nor windy suspiration of forc'd breath,

No, nor the fruitful river in the eye,

Nor the dejected havior of the visage,

Together with all forms, moods, shapes of grief,

'That can denote me truly. These indeed seem,

For they are actions that a man might play;

But I have that within which passeth show-

These but the trappings and the suits of woe.

King: 'Tis sweet and commendable in your nature, Hamlet,

To give these mourning duties to your father;

But you must know, your father lost a father;

That father lost, lost his, and the survivor bound

In filial obligation for some term

To do obsequious sorrow. But to persever

In obstinate condolement is a course

Of impious stubbornness. 'Tis unmanly grief;

It shows a will most incorrect to heaven,

A heart unfortified, a mind impatient,

An understanding simple and unschool'd;

For what we know must be, and is as common

As any the most vulgar thing to sense,
Why should we in our peevish opposition
Take it to heart? Fie! 'tis a fault to heaven,
A fault against the dead, a fault to nature,
To reason most absurd, whose common theme
Is death of fathers, and who still hath cried,
From the first corse till he that died to-day,
'This must be so.' We pray you throw to earth
This unprevailing woe, and think of us
As of a father; for let the world take note
You are the most immediate to our throne,
And with no less nobility of love
Than that which dearest father bears his son
Do I impart toward you. For your intent
In going back to school in Wittenberg,
It is most retrograde to our desire;
And we beseech you, bend you to remain
Here in the cheer and comfort of our eye,
Our chiefest courtier, cousin, and our son.

Queen: Let not thy mother lose her prayers, Hamlet.
I pray thee stay with us, go not to Wittenberg.

Hamlet: I shall in all my best obey you, madam.

King: Why, 'tis a loving and a fair reply.

Be as ourself in Denmark. Madam, come.

This gentle and unforc'd accord of Hamlet

Sits smiling to my heart; in grace whereof,

No jocund health that Denmark drinks to-day

But the great cannon to the clouds shall tell,

And the King's rouse the heaven shall bruit again,

Respeaking earthly thunder. Come away.

[Flourish. Exeunt all but Hamlet.]

Hamlet: O that this too too solid flesh would melt,

Thaw, and resolve itself into a dew!

Or that the Everlasting had not fix'd

His canon 'gainst self-slaughter! O God! God!

How weary, stale, flat, and unprofitable

Seem to me all the uses of this world!

Fie on't! ah, fie! 'Tis an unweeded garden

That grows to seed; things rank and gross in nature

Possess it merely. That it should come to this!

But two months dead! Nay, not so much, not two.

So excellent a king, that was to this

Hyperion to a satyr; so loving to my mother

That he might not beteem the winds of heaven

Visit her face too roughly. Heaven and earth!
Must I remember? Why, she would hang on him
As if increase of appetite had grown
By what it fed on; and yet, within a month-
Let me not think on't! Frailty, thy name is
woman!-
A little month, or ere those shoes were old
With which she followed my poor father's body
Like Niobe, all tears- why she, even she
(O God! a beast that wants discourse of reason
Would have mourn'd longer) married with my
uncle;
My father's brother, but no more like my father
Than I to Hercules. Within a month,
Ere yet the salt of most unrighteous tears
Had left the flushing in her galled eyes,
She married. O, most wicked speed, to post
With such dexterity to incestuous sheets!
It is not, nor it cannot come to good.
But break my heart, for I must hold my tongue!
[Enter Horatio, Marcellus, and Bernardo.]
Horatio: Hail to your lordship!
Hamlet: I am glad to see you well.
Horatio!- or I do forget myself.

Horatio: The same, my lord, and your poor servant ever.

Hamlet: Sir, my good friend- I'll change that name with you.

And what make you from Wittenberg, Horatio? Marcellus?

Marcellus: My good lord!

Hamlet: I am very glad to see you.- [To Bernardo] Good even, sir.-

But what, in faith, make you from Wittenberg?

Horatio: A truant disposition, good my lord.

Hamlet: I would not hear your enemy say so,

Nor shall you do my ear that violence

To make it truster of your own report

Against yourself. I know you are no truant.

But what is your affair in Elsinore?

We'll teach you to drink deep ere you depart.

Horatio: My lord, I came to see your father's funeral.

Hamlet: I prithee do not mock me, fellow student.

I think it was to see my mother's wedding.

Horatio: Indeed, my lord, it followed hard upon.

Hamlet: Thrift, thrift, Horatio! The funeral bak'd

meats

Did coldly furnish forth the marriage tables.

Would I had met my dearest foe in heaven

Or ever I had seen that day, Horatio!

My father- methinks I see my father.

Horatio: O, where, my lord?

Hamlet: In my mind's eye, Horatio.

Horatio: I saw him once. He was a goodly King.

Hamlet: He was a man, take him for all in all.

I shall not look upon his like again.

Horatio: My lord, I think I saw him yesternight.

Hamlet: Saw? who?

Horatio: My lord, the King your father.

Hamlet: The King, my father?

Horatio: Season your admiration for a while

With an attent ear, till I may deliver

Upon the witness of these gentlemen,

This marvel to you.

Hamlet: For God's love let me hear!

Horatio: Two nights together had these gentlemen

Marcellus and Bernardo, on their watch

In the dead vast and middle of the night

Been thus encount'red. A figure like your father,

Armed at point exactly, cap-a-pe,

Appears before them and with solemn march

Goes slow and stately by them. Thrice he walk'd

By their oppress'd and fear-surprised eyes,

Within his truncheon's length; whilst they distill'd

Almost to jelly with the act of fear,

Stand dumb and speak not to him. This to me

In dreadful secrecy impart they did,

And I with them the third night kept the watch;

Where, as they had deliver'd, both in time,

Form of the thing, each word made true and

good,

The apparition comes. I knew your father.

These hands are not more like.

Hamlet: But where was this?

Marcellus: My lord, upon the platform where we

watch'd.

Hamlet: Did you not speak to it?

Horatio: My lord, I did;

But answer made it none. Yet once methought

It lifted up it head and did address

Itself to motion, like as it would speak;

But even then the morning cock crew loud,

And at the sound it shrunk in haste away

And vanish'd from our sight.

Hamlet: 'Tis very strange.

Horatio: As I do live, my honour'd lord, 'tis true;
And we did think it writ down in our duty
To let you know of it.

Hamlet: Indeed, indeed, sirs. But this troubles me.
Hold you the watch to-night?

Marcellus and Bernardo: We do, my lord.

Hamlet: Arm'd, say you?

Both: Arm'd, my lord.

Hamlet: From top to toe?

Both: My lord, from head to foot.

Hamlet: Then saw you not his face?

Horatio: O, yes, my lord! He wore his beaver up.

Hamlet: What, look'd he frowningly.

Horatio: A countenance more in sorrow than in anger.

Hamlet: Pale or red?

Horatio: Nay, very pale.

Hamlet: And fix'd his eyes upon you?

Horatio: Most constantly.

Hamlet: I would I had been there.

Horatio: It would have much amaz'd you.

Hamlet: Very like, very like. Stay'd it long?

Horatio: While one with moderate haste might tell a hundred.

Both: Longer, longer.

Horatio: Not when I saw't.

Hamlet: His beard was grizzled- no?

Horatio: It was, as I have seen it in his life, A sable silver'd.

Hamlet: I will watch to-night. Perchance 'twill walk again.

Horatio: I warr'nt it will.

Hamlet: If it assume my noble father's person, I'll speak to it, though hell itself should gape And bid me hold my peace. I pray you all, If you have hitherto conceal'd this sight, Let it be tenable in your silence still; And whatsoever else shall hap to-night, Give it an understanding but no tongue. I will requite your loves. So, fare you well. Upon the platform, 'twixt eleven and twelve, I'll visit you.

All: Our duty to your honour.

Hamlet: Your loves, as mine to you. Farewell.

[Exeunt all but Hamlet.]

My father's spirit- in arms? All is not well.

I doubt some foul play. Would the night were

come!

Till then sit still, my soul. Foul deeds will rise,

Though all the earth o'erwhelm them, to men's

eyes.

  [Exit.]

Scene III - Elsinore. A room in Polonius' house.

- Laertes warns ophelia not to fall in love with Hamlet - because of class.

[Enter Laertes and Ophelia.]

Laertes: My necessaries are embark'd. Farewell.

And, sister, as the winds give benefit

And convoy is assistant, do not sleep,

But let me hear from you.

Ophelia: Do you doubt that?

Laertes: For Hamlet, and the trifling of his

favour,

Hold it a fashion, and a toy in blood; *premose*

A violet in the youth of primy nature,

Forward, not permanent- sweet, not lasting;

The perfume and suppliance of a minute;

No more.

foreshadowing ophelias drowning

Ophelia: No more but so?

Laertes: Think it no more.

For nature, crescent, does not grow alone

In thews and bulk; but as this temple waxes,

The inward service of the mind and soul

Grows wide withal. Perhaps he loves you now,

And now no soil nor cautel doth besmirch

The virtue of his will; but you must fear,

His greatness weigh'd, his will is not his own;

For he himself is subject to his birth.

He may not, as unvalued persons do,

Carve for himself, for on his choice depends

The safety and health of this whole state,

And therefore must his choice be circumscrib'd

Unto the voice and yielding of that body

Whereof he is the head. Then if he says he loves

you,

It fits your wisdom so far to believe it

As he in his particular act and place

May give his saying deed; which is no further

Than the main voice of Denmark goes withal.

Then weigh what loss your honour may sustain

If with too credent ear you list his songs,

Or lose your heart, or your chaste treasure open

To his unmast'red importunity.

Fear it, Ophelia, fear it, my dear sister,

And keep you in the rear of your affection,

Out of the shot and danger of desire.

The chariest maid is prodigal enough

If she unmask her beauty to the moon.

Virtue itself scopes not calumnious strokes.

The canker galls the infants of the spring

Too oft before their buttons be disclos'd,

And in the morn and liquid dew of youth

Contagious blastments are most imminent.

Be wary then; best safety lies in fear.

Youth to itself rebels, though none else near.

Ophelia: I shall th' effect of this good lesson keep

As watchman to my heart. But, good my brother,

Do not as some ungracious pastors do,

Show me the steep and thorny way to heaven,

Whiles, like a puff'd and reckless libertine,

Himself the primrose path of dalliance treads

And recks not his own rede.

Laertes: O, fear me not!

[Enter Polonius.]

I stay too long. But here my father comes.

A double blessing is a double grace;

Occasion smiles upon a second leave.

Polonius: Yet here, Laertes? Aboard, aboard,
for shame!

The wind sits in the shoulder of your sail,

And you are stay'd for. There- my blessing with
thee!

And these few precepts in thy memory

Look thou character. Give thy thoughts no
tongue,

Nor any unproportion'd thought his act.

Be thou familiar, but by no means vulgar:

Those friends thou hast, and their adoption tried,

Grapple them unto thy soul with hoops of steel;

But do not dull thy palm with entertainment

Of each new-hatch'd, unfledg'd comrade.
Beware

Of entrance to a quarrel; but being in,

Bear't that th' opposed may beware of thee.

Give every man thine ear, but few thy voice;

Take each man's censure, but reserve thy
judgment.

Costly thy habit as thy purse can buy,

But not express'd in fancy; rich, not gaudy;

For the apparel oft proclaims the man,

And they in France of the best rank and station

Are most select and generous, chief in that.

Neither a borrower nor a lender be;

For loan oft loses both itself and friend,

And borrowing dulls the edge of husbandry.

This above all- to thine own self be true,

And it must follow, as the night the day,

Thou canst not then be false to any man.

Farewell. My blessing season this in thee!

Laertes: Most humbly do I take my leave, my lord.

Polonius: The time invites you. Go, your servants tend.

Laertes: Farewell, Ophelia, and remember well What I have said to you.

Ophelia: 'Tis in my memory lock'd, And you yourself shall keep the key of it.

Laertes: Farewell.

[Exit.]

Polonius: What is't, Ophelia, he hath said to you?

Ophelia: So please you, something touching the Lord Hamlet.

Polonius: Marry, well bethought!

'Tis told me he hath very oft of late

Given private time to you, and you yourself

Have of your audience been most free and

bounteous.

If it be so- as so 'tis put on me,

And that in way of caution- I must tell you

You do not understand yourself so clearly

As it behooves my daughter and your honour.

What is between you? Give me up the truth.

Ophelia: He hath, my lord, of late made many

tenders

Of his affection to me.

Polonius: Affection? Pooh! You speak like a

green girl,

Unsifted in such perilous circumstance.

Do you believe his tenders, as you call them?

Ophelia: I do not know, my lord, what I should

think,

Polonius: Marry, I will teach you! Think yourself

a baby

That you have ta'en these tenders for true pay,

Which are not sterling. Tender yourself more

dearly,

Or (not to crack the wind of the poor phrase,
Running it thus) you'll tender me a fool.

Ophelia: My lord, he hath importun'd me with
love
In honourable fashion.

Polonius: Ay, fashion you may call it. Go to, go
to!

Ophelia: And hath given countenance to his
speech, my lord,
With almost all the holy vows of heaven.

Polonius: Ay, springes to catch woodcocks! I do
know,
When the blood burns, how prodigal the soul
Lends the tongue vows. These blazes, daughter,
Giving more light than heat, extinct in both
Even in their promise, as it is a-making,
You must not take for fire. From this time
Be something scanter of your maiden presence.
Set your entreatments at a higher rate
Than a command to parley. For Lord Hamlet,
Believe so much in him, that he is young,
And with a larger tether may he walk
Than may be given you. In few, Ophelia,
Do not believe his vows; for they are brokers,

Not of that dye which their investments show,

But mere implorators of unholy suits,

Breathing like sanctified and pious bawds,

The better to beguile. This is for all:

I would not, in plain terms, from this time forth

Have you so slander any moment leisure

As to give words or talk with the Lord Hamlet.

Look to't, I charge you. Come your ways.

Ophelia: I shall obey, my lord.

[Exeunt.]

Scene IV - Elsinore. The platform before the Castle.

[Enter Hamlet, Horatio, and Marcellus.]

Hamlet: The air bites shrewdly; it is very cold.

Horatio: It is a nipping and an eager air.

Hamlet: What hour now?

Horatio: I think it lacks of twelve.

Marcellus: No, it is struck.

Horatio: Indeed? I heard it not. It then draws near the season

Wherein the spirit held his wont to walk.

A flourish of trumpets, and two pieces go off.

What does this mean, my lord?

Hamlet: The King doth wake to-night and takes his rouse,

Keeps wassail, and the swagg'ring upspring reels,

And, as he drains his draughts of Rhenish down,

The kettledrum and trumpet thus bray out

The triumph of his pledge.

Horatio: Is it a custom?

Hamlet: Ay, marry, is't;

But to my mind, though I am native here

And to the manner born, it is a custom

More honour'd in the breach than the observance.

This heavy-headed revel east and west

Makes us traduced and taxed of other nations;

They clepe us drunkards and with swinish phrase

Soil our addition; and indeed it takes

From our achievements, though performed at height,

The pith and marrow of our attribute.

So oft it chances in particular men

That, for some vicious mole of nature in them,

As in their birth,- wherein they are not guilty,

Since nature cannot choose his origin,-

By the o'ergrowth of some complexion,

Oft breaking down the pales and forts of reason,

Or by some habit that too much o'erleavens

The form of plausive manners, that these men

Carrying, I say, the stamp of one defect,

Being nature's livery, or fortune's star,

Their virtues else- be they as pure as grace,

As infinite as man may undergo-

Shall in the general censure take corruption

From that particular fault. The dram of evil

Doth all the noble substance of a doubt To his

own scandal.

[Enter Ghost.]

Horatio: Look, my lord, it comes!

Hamlet: Angels and ministers of grace defend

us!

Be thou a spirit of health or goblin damn'd,

Bring with thee airs from heaven or blasts from

hell,

Be thy intents wicked or charitable,

Thou com'st in such a questionable shape

That I will speak to thee. I'll call thee Hamlet,

King, father, royal Dane. O, answer me?
Let me not burst in ignorance, but tell
Why thy canoniz'd bones, hearsed in death,
Have burst their cerements; why the sepulchre
Wherein we saw thee quietly inurn'd,
Hath op'd his ponderous and marble jaws
To cast thee up again. What may this mean
That thou, dead corse, again in complete steel,
Revisits thus the glimpses of the moon,
Making night hideous, and we fools of nature
So horridly to shake our disposition
With thoughts beyond the reaches of our souls?
Say, why is this? wherefore? What should we
do?
[Ghost beckons Hamlet.]
Horatio: It beckons you to go away with it,
As if it some impartment did desire
To you alone.
Marcellus: Look with what courteous action
It waves you to a more removed ground.
But do not go with it!
Horatio: No, by no means!
Hamlet: It will not speak. Then will I follow it.
Horatio: Do not, my lord!

Hamlet: Why, what should be the fear?

I do not set my life at a pin's fee;

And for my soul, what can it do to that,

Being a thing immortal as itself?

It waves me forth again. I'll follow it.

Horatio: What if it tempt you toward the flood,

my lord,

Or to the dreadful summit of the cliff

That beetles o'er his base into the sea,

And there assume some other, horrible form

Which might deprive your sovereignty of reason

And draw you into madness? Think of it.

The very place puts toys of desperation,

Without more motive, into every brain

That looks so many fathoms to the sea

And hears it roar beneath.

Hamlet: It waves me still.

Go on. I'll follow thee.

Marcellus: You shall not go, my lord.

Hamlet: Hold off your hands!

Horatio: Be rul'd. You shall not go.

Hamlet: My fate cries out

And makes each petty artere in this body

As hardy as the Nemean lion's nerve.

[Ghost beckons.]

Still am I call'd. Unhand me, gentlemen.

By heaven, I'll make a ghost of him that lets me!-

I say, away!- Go on. I'll follow thee.

[Exeunt Ghost and Hamlet.]

Horatio: He waxes desperate with imagination.

Marcellus: Let's follow. 'Tis not fit thus to obey him.

Horatio: Have after. To what issue wail this come?

Marcellus: Something is rotten in the state of Denmark.

Horatio: Heaven will direct it.

Marcellus: Nay, let's follow him.

[Exeunt.]

Scene V - Elsinore. The Castle. Another part of the fortifications.

[Enter Ghost and Hamlet.]

Hamlet: Whither wilt thou lead me? Speak! I'll go no further.

Ghost: Mark me.

Hamlet: I will.

Ghost: My hour is almost come,

When I to sulph'rous and tormenting flames

Must render up myself.

Hamlet: Alas, poor ghost!

Ghost: Pity me not, but lend thy serious hearing

To what I shall unfold.

Hamlet: Speak. I am bound to hear.

Ghost: So art thou to revenge, when thou shalt

hear.

Hamlet: What?

Ghost: I am thy father's spirit,

Doom'd for a certain term to walk the night,

And for the day confin'd to fast in fires, ~ Hell

Till the foul crimes done in my days of nature

Are burnt and purg'd away. But that I am forbid

To tell the secrets of my prison house,

I could a tale unfold whose lightest word

Would harrow up thy soul, freeze thy young

blood,

Make thy two eyes, like stars, start from their

spheres,

Thy knotted and combined locks to part,

And each particular hair to stand an end

Like quills upon the fretful porpentine.

But this eternal blazon must not be

To ears of flesh and blood. List, list, O, list!

If thou didst ever thy dear father love-

Hamlet: O God!

Ghost: Revenge his foul and most unnatural

murder.

Hamlet: Murder?

Ghost: Murder most foul, as in the best it is;

But this most foul, strange, and unnatural.

Hamlet: Haste me to know't, that I, with wings as

swift

As meditation or the thoughts of love,

May sweep to my revenge.

Ghost: I find thee apt;

And duller shouldst thou be than the fat weed

That rots itself in ease on Lethe wharf,

Wouldst thou not stir in this. Now, Hamlet, hear.

'Tis given out that, sleeping in my orchard,

A serpent stung me. So the whole ear of

Denmark

Is by a forged process of my death

Rankly abus'd. But know, thou noble youth,

The serpent that did sting thy father's life

Now wears his crown.

Garden
g eden

Metaphor for Hamlet Uncle - new
king

Hamlet: O my prophetic soul!

My uncle?

Ghost: Ay, that incestuous, that adulterate
beast,

With witchcraft of his wit, with traitorous gifts-

O wicked wit and gifts, that have the power

So to seduce!- won to his shameful lust

The will of my most seeming-virtuous Queen.

O Hamlet, what a falling-off was there,

From me, whose love was of that dignity

That it went hand in hand even with the vow

I made to her in marriage, and to decline

Upon a wretch whose natural gifts were poor

To those of mine!

But virtue, as it never will be mov'd,

Though lewdness court it in a shape of heaven,

So lust, though to a radiant angel link'd,

Will sate itself in a celestial bed

And prey on garbage.

But soft! methinks I scent the morning air.

Brief let me be. Sleeping within my orchard,

My custom always of the afternoon,

Upon my secure hour thy uncle stole,

With juice of cursed hebona in a vial,

And in the porches of my ears did pour

The leperous distilment; whose effect

Holds such an enmity with blood of man

That swift as quicksilver it courses through

The natural gates and alleys of the body,

And with a sudden vigour it doth posset

And curd, like eager droppings into milk,

The thin and wholesome blood. So did it mine;

And a most instant tetter bark'd about,

Most lazar-like, with vile and loathsome crust

All my smooth body.

Thus was I, sleeping, by a brother's hand

Of life, of crown, of queen, at once dispatch'd;

Cut off even in the blossoms of my sin,

Unhous'led, disappointed, unanel'd,

No reckoning made, but sent to my account

With all my imperfections on my head.

Hamlet: O, horrible! O, horrible! most horrible!

Ghost: If thou hast nature in thee, bear it not.

Let not the royal bed of Denmark be

A couch for luxury and damned incest.

But, howsoever thou pursuest this act,

Taint not thy mind, nor let thy soul contrive

Against thy mother aught. Leave her to heaven,

[handwritten annotations: "distressed", "exclemadore prince"]

And to those thorns that in her bosom lodge

To prick and sting her. Fare thee well at once.

The glow-worm shows the matin to be near

And gins to pale his uneffectual fire.

Adieu, adieu, adieu! Remember me.

[Exit.]

Hamlet: O all you host of heaven! O earth! What else?

And shall I couple hell? Hold, hold, my heart!

And you, my sinews, grow not instant old,

But bear me stiffly up. Remember thee?

Ay, thou poor ghost, while memory holds a seat

In this distracted globe. Remember thee?

Yea, from the table of my memory

I'll wipe away all trivial fond records,

All saws of books, all forms, all pressures past

That youth and observation copied there,

And thy commandment all alone shall live

Within the book and volume of my brain,

Unmix'd with baser matter. Yes, by heaven!

O most pernicious woman!

O villain, villain, smiling, damned villain!

My tables! Meet it is I set it down

That one may smile, and smile, and be a villain;

At least I am sure it may be so in Denmark.

[Writes.]

So, uncle, there you are. Now to my word:

It is 'Adieu, adieu! Remember me.'

I have sworn't.

Horatio: [within] My lord, my lord!

[Enter Horatio and Marcellus.]

Marcellus: Lord Hamlet!

Horatio: Heaven secure him!

Hamlet: So be it!

Marcellus: Hillo, ho, ho, my lord!

Hamlet: Hillo, ho, ho, boy! Come, bird, come.

Marcellus: How is't, my noble lord?

Horatio: What news, my lord?

Marcellus: O, wonderful!

Horatio: Good my lord, tell it.

Hamlet: No, you will reveal it.

Horatio: Not I, my lord, by heaven!

Marcellus: Nor I, my lord.

Hamlet: How say you then? Would heart of man once think it?

But you'll be secret?

Both: Ay, by heaven, my lord.

Hamlet: There's neer a villain dwelling in all

Denmark

But he's an arrant knave.

Horatio: There needs no ghost, my lord, come from the grave

To tell us this.

Hamlet: Why, right! You are in the right!

And so, without more circumstance at all,

I hold it fit that we shake hands and part;

You, as your business and desires shall point you,

For every man hath business and desire,

Such as it is; and for my own poor part,

Look you, I'll go pray.

Horatio: These are but wild and whirling words, my lord.

Hamlet: I am sorry they offend you, heartily;

Yes, faith, heartily.

Horatio: There's no offence, my lord.

Hamlet: Yes, by Saint Patrick, but there is, Horatio,

And much offence too. Touching this vision here,

It is an honest ghost, that let me tell you.

For your desire to know what is between us,

O'ermaster't as you may. And now, good friends,

As you are friends, scholars, and soldiers,

Give me one poor request.

Horatio: What is't, my lord? We will.

Hamlet: Never make known what you have seen
to-night.

Both: My lord, we will not.

Hamlet: Nay, but swear't.

Horatio: In faith,

My lord, not I.

Marcellus: Nor I, my lord- in faith.

Hamlet: Upon my sword.

Marcellus: We have sworn, my lord, already.

Hamlet: Indeed, upon my sword, indeed.

[Ghost cries under the stage.]

Ghost: Swear.

Hamlet: Aha boy, say'st thou so? Art thou there,
truepenny?

Come on! You hear this fellow in the cellarage.

Consent to swear.

Horatio: Propose the oath, my lord.

Hamlet: Never to speak of this that you have
seen.

Swear by my sword.

Ghost: [beneath] Swear.

Hamlet: *Hic et ubique*? Then we'll shift our ground.

Come hither, gentlemen,

And lay your hands again upon my sword.

Never to speak of this that you have heard:

Swear by my sword.

Ghost: [beneath] Swear by his sword.

Hamlet: Well said, old mole! Canst work i' th' earth so fast?

A worthy pioneer! Once more remove, good friends."

Horatio: O day and night, but this is wondrous strange!

Hamlet: And therefore as a stranger give it welcome.

There are more things in heaven and earth, Horatio,

Than are dreamt of in your philosophy.

But come!

Here, as before, never, so help you mercy,

How strange or odd soe'er I bear myself

(As I perchance hereafter shall think meet

To put an antic disposition on),

That you, at such times seeing me, never shall,

With arms encumb'red thus, or this head-shake,

Or by pronouncing of some doubtful phrase,

As 'Well, well, we know,' or 'We could, an if we
would,'

Or 'If we list to speak,' or 'There be, an if they
might,'

Or such ambiguous giving out, to note

That you know aught of me- this is not to do,

So grace and mercy at your most need help you,

Swear.

Ghost: [beneath] Swear.

[They swear.]

Hamlet: Rest, rest, perturbed spirit! So,
gentlemen,

With all my love I do commend me to you;

And what so poor a man as Hamlet is

May do t' express his love and friending to you,

God willing, shall not lack. Let us go in together;

And still your fingers on your lips, I pray.

The time is out of joint. O cursed spite

That ever I was born to set it right!

Nay, come, let's go together.

[Exeunt.]

My Notes

ACT II

Scene I - Elsinore. A room in Polonius' house.

[Enter Polonius and Reynaldo.]

Polonius: Give him this money and these notes, Reynaldo.

Reynaldo: I will, my lord.

Polonius: You shall do marvellous wisely, good Reynaldo,

Before You visit him, to make inquire

Of his behaviour.

Reynaldo: My lord, I did intend it.

Polonius: Marry, well said, very well said. Look you, sir,

Enquire me first what Danskers are in Paris;

And how, and who, what means, and where they keep,

What company, at what expense; and finding

By this encompassment and drift of question

That they do know my son, come you more nearer

Than your particular demands will touch it.

Take you, as 'twere, some distant knowledge of him;

As thus, 'I know his father and his friends,

And in part him.' Do you mark this, Reynaldo?

Reynaldo: Ay, very well, my lord.

Polonius: 'And in part him, but,' you may say, 'not well.

But if't be he I mean, he's very wild

Addicted so and so'; and there put on him

What forgeries you please; marry, none so rank

As may dishonour him- take heed of that;

But, sir, such wanton, wild, and usual slips

As are companions noted and most known

To youth and liberty.

Reynaldo: As gaming, my lord.

Polonius: Ay, or drinking, fencing, swearing, quarrelling,

Drabbing. You may go so far.

Reynaldo: My lord, that would dishonour him.

Polonius: Faith, no, as you may season it in the charge.

You must not put another scandal on him,

That he is open to incontinency.

That's not my meaning. But breathe his faults so

quaintly

That they may seem the taints of liberty,

The flash and outbreak of a fiery mind,

A savageness in unreclaimed blood,

Of general assault.

Reynaldo: But, my good lord-

Polonius: Wherefore should you do this?

Reynaldo: Ay, my lord,

I would know that.

Polonius: Marry, sir, here's my drift,

And I believe it is a fetch of warrant.

You laying these slight sullies on my son

As 'twere a thing a little soil'd i' th' working,

Mark you,

Your party in converse, him you would sound,

Having ever seen in the prenominate crimes

The youth you breathe of guilty, be assur'd

He closes with you in this consequence:

'Good sir,' or so, or 'friend,' or 'gentleman'-

According to the phrase or the addition

Of man and country-

Reynaldo: Very good, my lord.

Polonius: And then, sir, does 'a this- 'a does-

What was I about to say?

By the mass, I was about to say something!
Where did I leave?

Reynaldo: At 'closes in the consequence,' at
'friend or so,' and gentleman.'

Polonius: At 'closes in the consequence'- Ay,
marry!

He closes thus: 'I know the gentleman.

I saw him yesterday, or t'other day,

Or then, or then, with such or such; and, as you
say,

There was 'a gaming; there o'ertook in's rouse;

There falling out at tennis'; or perchance,

'I saw him enter such a house of sale,'

Videlicet, a brothel, or so forth.

See you now-

Your bait of falsehood takes this carp of truth;

And thus do we of wisdom and of reach,

With windlasses and with assays of bias,

By indirections find directions out.

So, by my former lecture and advice,

Shall you my son. You have me, have you not

Reynaldo: My lord, I have.

Polonius: God b' wi' ye, fare ye well!

Reynaldo: Good my lord!

[Going.]

Polonius: Observe his inclination in yourself.

Reynaldo: I shall, my lord.

Polonius: And let him ply his music.

Reynaldo: Well, my lord.

Polonius: Farewell!

[Exit Reynaldo. Enter Ophelia.]

How now, Ophelia? What's the matter?

Ophelia: O my lord, my lord, I have been so
affrighted!

Polonius: With what, i' th' name of God?

Ophelia: My lord, as I was sewing in my closet,

Lord Hamlet, with his doublet all unbrac'd,

No hat upon his head, his stockings foul'd,

Ungart'red, and down-gyved to his ankle;

Pale as his shirt, his knees knocking each other,

And with a look so piteous in purport

As if he had been loosed out of hell

To speak of horrors- he comes before me.

Polonius: Mad for thy love?

Ophelia: My lord, I do not know,

But truly I do fear it.

Polonius: What said he?

Ophelia: He took me by the wrist and held me

hard;

Then goes he to the length of all his arm,

And, with his other hand thus o'er his brow,

He falls to such perusal of my face

As he would draw it. Long stay'd he so.

At last, a little shaking of mine arm,

And thrice his head thus waving up and down,

He rais'd a sigh so piteous and profound

As it did seem to shatter all his bulk

And end his being. That done, he lets me go,

And with his head over his shoulder turn'd

He seem'd to find his way without his eyes,

For out o' doors he went without their help

And to the last bended their light on me.

Polonius: Come, go with me. I will go seek the

King.

This is the very ecstasy of love,

Whose violent property fordoes itself

And leads the will to desperate undertakings

As oft as any passion under heaven

That does afflict our natures. I am sorry.

What, have you given him any hard words of

late?

Ophelia: No, my good lord; but, as you did

command,

I did repel his letters and denied

His access to me.

Polonius: That hath made him mad.

I am sorry that with better heed and judgment

I had not quoted him. I fear'd he did but trifle

And meant to wrack thee; but beshrew my

jealousy!

By heaven, it is as proper to our age

To cast beyond ourselves in our opinions

As it is common for the younger sort

To lack discretion. Come, go we to the King.

This must be known; which, being kept close,

might move

More grief to hide than hate to utter love.

Come.

[Exeunt.]

Scene II - Elsinore. A room in the Castle.

[Enter King, Queen, Rosencrantz, Guildenstern

and Attendants.]

King: Welcome, dear Rosencrantz and

Guildenstern.

Moreover that we much did long to see you,

The need we have to use you did provoke

Our hasty sending. Something have you heard

Of Hamlet's transformation. So I call it,

Sith nor th' exterior nor the inward man

Resembles that it was. What it should be,

More than his father's death, that thus hath put him

So much from th' understanding of himself,

I cannot dream of. I entreat you both

That, being of so young clays brought up with him,

And since so neighbour'd to his youth and haviour,

That you vouchsafe your rest here in our court

Some little time; so by your companies

To draw him on to pleasures, and to gather

So much as from occasion you may glean,

Whether aught to us unknown afflicts him thus

That, open'd, lies within our remedy.

Queen: Good gentlemen, he hath much talk'd of you,

And sure I am two men there are not living

To whom he more adheres. If it will please you

To show us so much gentry and good will

As to expend your time with us awhile

For the supply and profit of our hope,

Your visitation shall receive such thanks

As fits a king's remembrance.

Rosencrantz: Both your Majesties

Might, by the sovereign power you have of us,

Put your dread pleasures more into command

Than to entreaty.

Guildenstern: But we both obey,

And here give up ourselves, in the full bent,

To lay our service freely at your feet,

To be commanded.

King: Thanks, Rosencrantz and gentle

Guildenstern.

Queen: Thanks, Guildenstern and gentle

Rosencrantz.

And I beseech you instantly to visit

My too much changed son.- Go, some of you,

And bring these gentlemen where Hamlet is.

Guildenstern: Heavens make our presence and

our practices

Pleasant and helpful to him!

Queen: Ay, amen!

[Exeunt Rosencrantz and Guildenstern, with some Attendants.]

[Enter Polonius.]

Polonius: Th' ambassadors from Norway, my good lord,

Are joyfully return'd.

King: Thou still hast been the father of good news.

Polonius: Have I, my lord? Assure you, my good liege,

I hold my duty as I hold my soul,

Both to my God and to my gracious king;

And I do think- or else this brain of mine

Hunts not the trail of policy so sure

As it hath us'd to do- that I have found

The very cause of Hamlet's lunacy.

King: O, speak of that! That do I long to hear.

Polonius: Give first admittance to th' ambassadors.

My news shall be the fruit to that great feast.

King: Thyself do grace to them, and bring them in.

[Exit Polonius.]

He tells me, my dear Gertrude, he hath found

The head and source of all your son's distemper.

Queen: I doubt it is no other but the main,

His father's death and our o'erhasty marriage.

King: Well, we shall sift him.

[Enter Polonius, Voltemand, and Cornelius.]

Welcome, my good friends.

Say, Voltemand, what from our brother Norway?

Voltemand: Most fair return of greetings and desires.

Upon our first, he sent out to suppress

His nephew's levies; which to him appear'd

To be a preparation 'gainst the Polack,

But better look'd into, he truly found

It was against your Highness; whereat griev'd,

That so his sickness, age, and impotence

Was falsely borne in hand, sends out arrests

On Fortinbras; which he, in brief, obeys,

Receives rebuke from Norway, and, in fine,

Makes vow before his uncle never more

To give th' assay of arms against your Majesty.

Whereon old Norway, overcome with joy,

Gives him three thousand crowns in annual fee

And his commission to employ those soldiers,

So levied as before, against the Polack;

With an entreaty, herein further shown,

[Gives a paper.]

That it might please you to give quiet pass

Through your dominions for this enterprise,

On such regards of safety and allowance

As therein are set down.

King: It likes us well;

And at our more consider'd time we'll read,

Answer, and think upon this business.

Meantime we thank you for your well-took labour.

Go to your rest; at night we'll feast together.

Most welcome home!

[Exeunt Ambassadors.]

Polonius: This business is well ended.

My liege, and madam, to expostulate

What majesty should be, what duty is,

Why day is day, night is night, and time is time.

Were nothing but to waste night, day, and time.

Therefore, since brevity is the soul of wit,

And tediousness the limbs and outward

flourishes,

I will be brief. Your noble son is mad.

Mad call I it; for, to define true madness,

What is't but to be nothing else but mad?

But let that go.

Queen: More matter, with less art.

Polonius: Madam, I swear I use no art at all.

That he is mad, 'tis true: 'tis true 'tis pity;

And pity 'tis 'tis true. A foolish figure!

But farewell it, for I will use no art.

Mad let us grant him then. And now remains

That we find out the cause of this effect-

Or rather say, the cause of this defect,

For this effect defective comes by cause.

Thus it remains, and the remainder thus.

Perpend.

I have a daughter (have while she is mine),

Who in her duty and obedience, mark,

Hath given me this. Now gather, and surmise.

[Reads the letter.]

   '*To the celestial, and my soul's idol, the most beautified*

   Ophelia,'-

That's an ill phrase, a vile phrase; 'beautified' is a vile phrase.

But you shall hear. Thus:

[Reads.]

   '*In her excellent white bosom, these, etc.*'

Queen: Came this from Hamlet to her?

Polonius: Good madam, stay awhile. I will be faithful.   [Reads.]

>*'Doubt thou the stars are fire;*
> *Doubt that the sun doth move;*
> *Doubt truth to be a liar;*
>   *But never doubt I love.*
>
>*'O dear Ophelia, I am ill at these numbers; I have not art to reckon my groans; but that I love thee best, O most best, believe it. Adieu.*
>
>*'Thine evermore, most dear lady, whilst this machine is to him,*
>
>   *HAMLET.'*

This, in obedience, hath my daughter shown me;
And more above, hath his solicitings,
As they fell out by time, by means, and place,
All given to mine ear.

King: But how hath she
Receiv'd his love?

Polonius: What do you think of me?

King: As of a man faithful and honourable.

Polonius: I would fain prove so. But what might you think,
When I had seen this hot love on the wing

(As I perceiv'd it, I must tell you that,

Before my daughter told me), what might you,

Or my dear Majesty your queen here, think,

If I had play'd the desk or table book,

Or given my heart a winking, mute and dumb,

Or look'd upon this love with idle sight?

What might you think? No, I went round to work

And my young mistress thus I did bespeak:

'Lord Hamlet is a prince, out of thy star.

This must not be.' And then I prescripts gave her,

That she should lock herself from his resort,

Admit no messengers, receive no tokens.

Which done, she took the fruits of my advice,

And he, repulsed, a short tale to make,

Fell into a sadness, then into a fast,

Thence to a watch, thence into a weakness,

Thence to a lightness, and, by this declension,

Into the madness wherein now he raves,

And all we mourn for.

King: Do you think 'tis this?

Queen: it may be, very like.

Polonius: Hath there been such a time- I would

fain know that-

That I have Positively said "Tis so,'

When it prov'd otherwise?

King: Not that I know.

Polonius: [points to his head and shoulder] Take this from this, if this be otherwise.

If circumstances lead me, I will find

Where truth is hid, though it were hid indeed

Within the centre.

King: How may we try it further?

Polonius: You know sometimes he walks four hours together

Here in the lobby.

Queen: So he does indeed.

Polonius: At such a time I'll loose my daughter to him.

Be you and I behind an arras then.

Mark the encounter. If he love her not,

And he not from his reason fall'n thereon

Let me be no assistant for a state,

But keep a farm and carters.

King: We will try it.

[Enter Hamlet, reading on a book.]

Queen: But look where sadly the poor wretch comes reading.

Polonius: Away, I do beseech you, both away

I'll board him presently. O, give me leave.

[Exeunt King and Queen, with Attendants.]

How does my good Lord Hamlet?

Hamlet: Well, God-a-mercy.

Polonius: Do you know me, my lord?

Hamlet: Excellent well. You are a fishmonger.

Polonius: Not I, my lord.

Hamlet: Then I would you were so honest a man.

Polonius: Honest, my lord?

Hamlet: Ay, sir. To be honest, as this world goes, is to be one man pick'd out of ten thousand.

Polonius: That's very true, my lord.

Hamlet: For if the sun breed maggots in a dead dog, being a god kissing carrion- Have you a daughter?

Polonius: I have, my lord.

Hamlet: Let her not walk i' th' sun. Conception is a blessing, but not as your daughter may conceive. Friend, look to't.

Polonius: [aside] How say you by that? Still harping on my daughter. Yet he knew me not at first. He said I was a fishmonger. He is far gone, far gone! And truly in my youth I suff'red much extremity for love- very near this. I'll speak to him again.- What do you read, my lord?

Hamlet: Words, words, words.

Polonius: What is the matter, my lord?

Hamlet: Between who?

Polonius: I mean, the matter that you read, my lord.

Hamlet: Slanders, sir; for the satirical rogue says here that old men have grey beards; that their faces are wrinkled; their eyes purging thick amber and plum-tree gum; and that they have a plentiful lack of wit, together with most weak hams. All which, sir, though I most powerfully and potently believe, yet I hold it not honesty to have it thus set down; for you yourself, sir, should be old as I am if, like a crab, you could go backward.

Polonius: [aside] Though this be madness, yet there is a method in't.-

Will you walk out of the air, my lord?

Hamlet: Into my grave?

Polonius: Indeed, that is out o' th' air. [Aside] How pregnant sometimes his replies are! a happiness that often madness hits on, which reason and sanity could not so prosperously be delivered of. I will leave him and suddenly contrive the means of meeting between him and my daughter.- My honourable lord, I will most humbly take my leave of you.

Hamlet: You cannot, sir, take from me anything that I will more willingly part withal- except my life, except my life, except my life,

[Enter Rosencrantz and Guildenstern.]

Polonius: Fare you well, my lord.

Hamlet: These tedious old fools!

Polonius: You go to seek the Lord Hamlet. There he is.

Rosencrantz: [to Polonius] God save you, sir!

[Exit Polonius.]

Guildenstern: My honour'd lord!

Rosencrantz: My most dear lord!

Hamlet: My excellent good friends! How dost thou, Guildenstern? Ah, Rosencrantz! Good lads, how do ye both?

Rosencrantz: As the indifferent children of the earth.

Guildenstern: Happy in that we are not over-happy.

On Fortune's cap we are not the very button.

Hamlet: Nor the soles of her shoe?

Rosencrantz: Neither, my lord.

Hamlet: Then you live about her waist, or in the middle of her favours?

Guildenstern: Faith, her privates we.

Hamlet: In the secret parts of Fortune? O! most true! she is a strumpet. What news?

Rosencrantz: None, my lord, but that the world's grown honest.

Hamlet: Then is doomsday near! But your news is not true. Let me question more in particular. What have you, my good friends, deserved at the hands of Fortune that she sends you to prison hither?

Guildenstern: Prison, my lord?

Hamlet: Denmark's a prison.

Rosencrantz: Then is the world one.

Hamlet: A goodly one; in which there are many confines, wards, and dungeons, Denmark being one o' th' worst.

Rosencrantz: We think not so, my lord.

Hamlet: Why, then 'tis none to you; for there is

nothing either good or bad but thinking makes it so. To me it is a prison.

Rosencrantz: Why, then your ambition makes it one. 'Tis too narrow for your mind.

Hamlet: O God, I could be bounded in a nutshell and count myself a king of infinite space, were it not that I have bad dreams.

Guildenstern: Which dreams indeed are ambition; for the very substance of the ambitious is merely the shadow of a dream.

Hamlet: A dream itself is but a shadow.

Rosencrantz: Truly, and I hold ambition of so airy and light a quality that it is but a shadow's shadow.

Hamlet: Then are our beggars bodies, and our monarchs and outstretch'd heroes the beggars' shadows. Shall we to th' court? for, by my fay, I cannot reason.

Both: We'll wait upon you.

Hamlet: No such matter! I will not sort you with the rest of my servants; for, to speak to you like an honest man, I am most dreadfully attended. But in the beaten way of friendship, what make you at Elsinore?

Rosencrantz: To visit you, my lord; no other occasion.

Hamlet: Beggar that I am, I am even poor in thanks; but I thank you; and sure, dear friends, my thanks are too dear a halfpenny. Were you not sent for? Is it your own inclining? Is it a free visitation? Come, deal justly with me. Come, come! Nay, speak.

Guildenstern: What should we say, my lord?

Hamlet: Why, anything- but to th' purpose. You were sent for; and there is a kind of confession in your looks, which your modesties have not craft enough to colour. I know the good King and Queen have sent for you.

Rosencrantz: To what end, my lord?

Hamlet: That you must teach me. But let me conjure you by the rights of our fellowship, by the consonancy of our youth, by the obligation of our ever-preserved love, and by what more dear a better proposer could charge you withal, be even and direct with me, whether you were sent for or no.

Rosencrantz: [aside to Guildenstern] What say you?

Hamlet: [aside] Nay then, I have an eye of you.-
If you love me, hold not off.

Guildenstern: My lord, we were sent for.

Hamlet: I will tell you why. So shall my
anticipation prevent your discovery, and your
secrecy to the King and Queen moult no feather.
I have of late- but wherefore I know not- lost all
my mirth, forgone all custom of exercises; and
indeed, it goes so heavily with my disposition
that this goodly frame, the earth, seems to me a
sterile promontory; this most excellent canopy,
the air, look you, this brave o'erhanging
firmament, this majestical roof fretted with golden
fire- why, it appeareth no other thing to me than
a foul and pestilent congregation of vapours.
What a piece of work is a man! how noble in
reason! how infinite in faculties! in form and
moving how express and admirable! In action
how like an angel! in apprehension how like a
god! The beauty of the world, the paragon of
animals! And yet to me what is this quintessence
of dust? Man delights not me- no, nor woman
neither, though by your smiling you seem to say
so.

Rosencrantz: My lord, there was no such stuff in my thoughts.

Hamlet: Why did you laugh then, when I said 'Man delights not me'?

Rosencrantz: To think, my lord, if you delight not in man, what lenten entertainment the players shall receive from you. We coted them on the way, and hither are they coming to offer you service.

Hamlet: He that plays the king shall be welcome- his Majesty shall have tribute of me; the adventurous knight shall use his foil and target; the lover shall not sigh gratis; the humorous man shall end his part in peace; the clown shall make those laugh whose lungs are tickle o' th' sere; and the lady shall say her mind freely, or the blank verse shall halt for 't. What players are they?

Rosencrantz: Even those you were wont to take such delight in, the tragedians of the city.

Hamlet: How chances it they travel? Their residence, both in reputation and profit, was better both ways.

Rosencrantz: I think their inhibition comes by

the means of the late innovation.

Hamlet: Do they hold the same estimation they did when I was in the city? Are they so follow'd?

Rosencrantz: No indeed are they not.

Hamlet: How comes it? Do they grow rusty?

Rosencrantz: Nay, their endeavour keeps in the wonted pace; but there is, sir, an eyrie of children, little eyases, that cry out on the top of question and are most tyrannically clapp'd fort. These are now the fashion, and so berattle the common stages (so they call them) that many wearing rapiers are afraid of goosequills and dare scarce come thither.

Hamlet: What, are they children? Who maintains 'em? How are they escoted? Will they pursue the quality no longer than they can sing? Will they not say afterwards, if they should grow themselves to common players (as it is most like, if their means are no better), their writers do them wrong to make them exclaim against their own succession.

Rosencrantz: Faith, there has been much to do on both sides; and the nation holds it no sin to tarre them to controversy. There was, for a while, no money bid for argument unless the poet and the player went to cuffs in the question.

Hamlet: Is't possible?

Guildenstern: O, there has been much throwing about of brains.

Hamlet: Do the boys carry it away?

Rosencrantz: Ay, that they do, my lord- Hercules and his load too.

Hamlet: It is not very strange; for my uncle is King of Denmark, and those that would make mows at him while my father lived give twenty, forty, fifty, a hundred ducats apiece for his picture in little. 'Sblood, there is something in this more than natural, if philosophy could find it out. [Flourish for the Players.]

Guildenstern: There are the players.

Hamlet: Gentlemen, you are welcome to Elsinore. Your hands, come! Th' appurtenance of welcome is fashion and ceremony. Let me comply with you in this garb, lest my extent to the players (which I tell you must show fairly outwards) should more appear like entertainment than yours. You are welcome. But my uncle-father and aunt-mother are deceiv'd.

Guildenstern: In what, my dear lord?

Hamlet: I am but mad north-north-west. When the wind is southerly I know a hawk from a handsaw.

[Enter Polonius.]

Polonius: Well be with you, gentlemen!

Hamlet: Hark you, Guildenstern- and you too- at each ear a hearer!

That great baby you see there is not yet out of his swaddling clouts.

Rosencrantz: Happily he's the second time come to them; for they say an old man is twice a child.

Hamlet: I will prophesy he comes to tell me of the players. Mark it.-

You say right, sir; a Monday morning; twas so indeed.

Polonius: My lord, I have news to tell you.

Hamlet: My lord, I have news to tell you. When Roscius was an actor in Rome-

Polonius: The actors are come hither, my lord.

Hamlet: Buzz, buzz!

Polonius: Upon my honour-

Hamlet: Then came each actor on his ass-

Polonius: The best actors in the world, either for tragedy, comedy, history, pastoral, pastoral-comical, historical-pastoral, tragical-historical, tragical-comical-historical-pastoral; scene individable, or poem unlimited. Seneca cannot be too heavy, nor Plautus too light. For the law of writ and the liberty, these are the only men.

Hamlet: O Jephthah, judge of Israel, what a treasure hadst thou!

Polonius: What treasure had he, my lord?

Hamlet: Why,

>   *'One fair daughter, and no more,*
>   *The which he loved passing well.'*

Polonius: [aside] Still on my daughter.

Hamlet: Am I not i' th' right, old Jephthah?

Polonius: If you call me Jephthah, my lord, I have a daughter that I love passing well.

Hamlet: Nay, that follows not.

Polonius: What follows then, my lord?

Hamlet: Why,

>   *'As by lot, God wot,'*

and then, you know,

>   *'It came to pass, as most like it was.'*

The first row of the pious chanson will show you

more; for look where my abridgment comes.
[Enter four or five Players.]
You are welcome, masters; welcome, all. I am glad to see thee well. Welcome, good friends. O, my old friend? Why, thy face I valanc'd since I saw thee last. Com'st' thou to' beard me in Denmark? What, my young lady and mistress? By'r Lady, your ladyship is nearer to heaven than when I saw you last by the altitude of a chopine. Pray God your voice, like a piece of uncurrent gold, be not crack'd within the ring.- Masters, you are all welcome. We'll e'en to't like French falconers, fly at anything we see. We'll have a speech straight. Come, give us a taste of your quality. Come, a passionate speech.

First Player: What speech, my good lord?

Hamlet: I heard thee speak me a speech once, but it was never acted; or if it was, not above once; for the play, I remember, pleas'd not the million, 'twas caviary to the general; but it was (as I receiv'd it, and others, whose judgments in such matters cried in the top of mine) an excellent play, well digested in the scenes, set down with as much modesty as cunning. I remember one said there were no sallets in the lines to make the matter savoury, nor no matter in the phrase that might indict the author of affectation; but call'd it an honest method, as wholesome as sweet, and by very much more handsome than fine. One speech in't I chiefly lov'd. 'Twas AEneas' tale to Dido, and thereabout of it especially where he speaks of Priam's slaughter. If it live in your memory, begin at this line- let me see, let me see:

'The rugged Pyrrhus, like th' Hyrcanian beast-'
'Tis not so; it begins with Pyrrhus:

'The rugged Pyrrhus, he whose sable arms,
Black as his purpose, did the night resemble
When he lay couched in the ominous horse,
Hath now this dread and black complexion smear'd
With heraldry more dismal. Head to foot
Now is be total gules, horridly trick'd
With blood of fathers, mothers, daughters, sons,
Bak'd and impasted with the parching streets,
That lend a tyrannous and a damned light
To their lord's murder. Roasted in wrath and

fire,

And thus o'ersized with coagulate gore,

With eyes like carbuncles, the hellish Pyrrhus

Old grandsire Priam seeks.'

So, proceed you.

Polonius: Fore God, my lord, well spoken, with good accent and good discretion.

First Player: *'Anon he finds him,*

Striking too short at Greeks. His antique sword,

Rebellious to his arm, lies where it falls,

Repugnant to command. Unequal match'd,

Pyrrhus at Priam drives, in rage strikes wide;

But with the whiff and wind of his fell sword

Th' unnerved father falls. Then senseless Ilium,

Seeming to feel this blow, with flaming top

Stoops to his base, and with a hideous crash

Takes prisoner Pyrrhus' ear. For lo! his sword,

Which was declining on the milky head

Of reverend Priam, seem'd i' th' air to stick.

So, as a painted tyrant, Pyrrhus stood,

And, like a neutral to his will and matter,

Did nothing.

But, as we often see, against some storm,

A silence in the heavens, the rack stand still,

The bold winds speechless, and the orb below

As hush as death- anon the dreadful thunder

Doth rend the region; so, after Pyrrhus' pause,

Aroused vengeance sets him new awork;

And never did the Cyclops' hammers fall

On Mars's armour, forg'd for proof eterne,

With less remorse than Pyrrhus' bleeding sword

Now falls on Priam.

Out, out, thou strumpet Fortune! All you gods,

In general synod take away her power;

Break all the spokes and fellies from her wheel,

And bowl the round nave down the hill of heaven,

As low as to the fiends!

Polonius: This is too long.

Hamlet: It shall to the barber's, with your beard.-

Prithee say on.

He's for a jig or a tale of bawdry, or he sleeps.

Say on;

come to Hecuba.

First Player: *'But who, O who, had seen the mobled queen-'*

Hamlet: *'The mobled queen'*?

Polonius: That's good! *'Mobled queen'* is good.

First Player: *'Run barefoot up and down, threat'ning the flames*

   With bisson rheum; a clout upon that head
   Where late the diadem stood, and for a robe,
   About her lank and all o'erteemed loins,
   A blanket, in the alarm of fear caught up-
   Who this had seen, with tongue in venom steep'd
   'Gainst Fortune's state would treason have pronounc'd.
   But if the gods themselves did see her then,
   When she saw Pyrrhus make malicious sport
   In Mincing with his sword her husband's limbs,
   The instant burst of clamour that she made
   (Unless things mortal move them not at all)
   Would have made milch the burning eyes of heaven
   And passion in the gods.'

Polonius: Look, whe'r he has not turn'd his colour, and has tears in's eyes. Prithee no more!

Hamlet: 'Tis well. I'll have thee speak out the rest of this soon. Good my lord, will you see the players well bestow'd? Do you hear? Let them be well us'd; for they are the abstract and brief chronicles of the time. After your death you were better have a bad epitaph than their ill report while you live.

Polonius: My lord, I will use them according to their desert.

Hamlet: God's bodykins, man, much better! Use every man after his desert, and who should scape whipping? Use them after your own honour and dignity. The less they deserve, the more merit is in your bounty. Take them in.

Polonius: Come, sirs.

Hamlet: Follow him, friends. We'll hear a play to-morrow.

[Exeunt Polonius and Players except the First].
Dost thou hear me, old friend? Can you play 'The Murder of Gonzago'?

First Player: Ay, my lord.

Hamlet: We'll ha't to-morrow night. You could, for a need, study a speech of some dozen or sixteen lines which I would set down and insert in't, could you not?

First Player: Ay, my lord.

Hamlet: Very well. Follow that lord- and look you mock him not.

[Exit First Player.]

My good friends, I'll leave you till night. You are welcome to

Elsinore.

Rosencrantz: Good my lord!

Hamlet: Ay, so, God b' wi' ye!

[Exeunt Rosencrantz and Guildenstern.]

Now I am alone.

O what a rogue and peasant slave am I!

Is it not monstrous that this player here,

But in a fiction, in a dream of passion,

Could force his soul so to his own conceit

That, from her working, all his visage wann'd,

Tears in his eyes, distraction in's aspect,

A broken voice, and his whole function suiting

With forms to his conceit? And all for nothing!

For Hecuba!

What's Hecuba to him, or he to Hecuba,

That he should weep for her? What would he do,

Had he the motive and the cue for passion

That I have? He would drown the stage with

tears

And cleave the general ear with horrid speech;

Make mad the guilty and appal the free,

Confound the ignorant, and amaze indeed

The very faculties of eyes and ears.

Yet I,

A dull and muddy-mettled rascal, peak

Like John-a-dreams, unpregnant of my cause,

And can say nothing! No, not for a king,

Upon whose property and most dear life

A damn'd defeat was made. Am I a coward?

Who calls me villain? breaks my pate across,

Plucks off my beard and blows it in my face,

Tweaks me by th' nose? gives me the lie i' th'

throat

As deep as to the lungs? Who does me this, ha?

'Swounds, I should take it! for it cannot be

But I am pigeon-livered and lack gall

To make oppression bitter, or ere this

I should have fatted all the region kites

With this slave's offal. Bloody bawdy villain!

Remorseless, treacherous, lecherous, kindless

villain!

O, vengeance!

Why, what an ass am I! This is most brave,

That I, the son of a dear father murder'd,

Prompted to my revenge by heaven and hell,

Must (like a whore) unpack my heart with words

And fall a-cursing like a very drab,

A scullion!

Fie upon't! foh! About, my brain! Hum, I have heard

That guilty creatures, sitting at a play,

Have by the very cunning of the scene

Been struck so to the soul that presently

They have proclaim'd their malefactions;

For murder, though it have no tongue, will speak

With most miraculous organ, I'll have these Players

Play something like the murder of my father

Before mine uncle. I'll observe his looks;

I'll tent him to the quick. If he but blench,

I know my course. The spirit that I have seen

May be a devil; and the devil hath power

T' assume a pleasing shape; yea, and perhaps

Out of my weakness and my melancholy,

As he is very potent with such spirits,

Abuses me to damn me. I'll have grounds

More relative than this. The play's the thing

Wherein I'll catch the conscience of the King.

[Exit.]

My Notes

ACT III

Scene I - Elsinore. A room in the Castle.

[Enter King, Queen, Polonius, Ophelia,
Rosencrantz, Guildenstern and Lords.]

King: And can you by no drift of conference

Get from him why he puts on this confusion,

Grating so harshly all his days of quiet

With turbulent and dangerous lunacy?

Rosencrantz: He does confess he feels himself

distracted,

But from what cause he will by no means speak.

Guildenstern: Nor do we find him forward to be

sounded,

But with a crafty madness keeps aloof

When we would bring him on to some confession

Of his true state.

Queen: Did he receive you well?

Rosencrantz: Most like a gentleman.

Guildenstern: But with much forcing of his

disposition.

Rosencrantz: Niggard of question, but of our

demands

Most free in his reply.

Queen: Did you assay him

To any pastime?

Rosencrantz: Madam, it so fell out that certain

players

We o'erraught on the way. Of these we told him,

And there did seem in him a kind of joy

To hear of it. They are here about the court,

And, as I think, they have already order

This night to play before him.

Polonius: 'Tis most true;

And he beseech'd me to entreat your Majesties

To hear and see the matter.

King: With all my heart, and it doth much content

me

To hear him so inclin'd.

Good gentlemen, give him a further edge

And drive his purpose on to these delights.

Rosencrantz: We shall, my lord.

[Exeunt Rosencrantz and Guildenstern.]

King: Sweet Gertrude, leave us too;

For we have closely sent for Hamlet hither,

That he, as 'twere by accident, may here

Affront Ophelia.

Her father and myself, lawful espials

Will so bestow ourselves that, seeing unseen,

We may of their encounter frankly judge

And gather by him, as he is behav'd,

If't be th' affliction of his love, or no,

That thus he suffers for.

Queen: I shall obey you;

And for your part, Ophelia, I do wish

That your good beauties be the happy cause

Of Hamlet's wildness. So shall I hope your

virtues

Will bring him to his wonted way again,

To both your honours.

Ophelia: Madam, I wish it may.

[Exit Queen.]

Polonius: Ophelia, walk you here.- Gracious, so

please you,

We will bestow ourselves. Read on this book,

That show of such an exercise may colour

Your loneliness. We are oft to blame in this,

'Tis too much prov'd, that with devotion's visage

And pious action we do sugar o'er

The Devil himself.

King: [aside] O, 'tis too true!

How smart a lash that speech doth give my
conscience!

The harlot's cheek, beautied with plast'ring art,

Is not more ugly to the thing that helps it

Than is my deed to my most painted word.

O heavy burden!

Polonius: I hear him coming. Let's withdraw, my
lord.

[Exeunt King and Polonius].

[Enter Hamlet.]

Hamlet: To be, or not to be- that is the question:

Whether 'tis nobler in the mind to suffer

The slings and arrows of outrageous fortune

Or to take arms against a sea of troubles,

And by opposing end them. To die- to sleep-

No more; and by a sleep to say we end

The heartache, and the thousand natural shocks

That flesh is heir to. 'Tis a consummation

Devoutly to be wish'd. To die, to sleep.

To sleep, perchance to dream: ay, there's the
rub!

For in that sleep of death what dreams may
come

When we have shuffled off this mortal coil,

Must give us pause. There's the respect

That makes calamity of so long life.

For who would bear the whips and scorns of

time,

Th' oppressor's wrong, the proud man's

contumely,

The pangs of despis'd love, the law's delay,

The insolence of office, and the spurns

That patient merit of th' unworthy takes,

When he himself might his quietus make

With a bare bodkin? Who would these fardels

bear,

To grunt and sweat under a weary life,

But that the dread of something after death-

The undiscover'd country, from whose bourn

No traveller returns, puzzles the will,

And makes us rather bear those ills we have

Than fly to others that we know not of?

Thus conscience does make cowards of us all,

And thus the native hue of resolution

Is sicklied o'er with the pale cast of thought,

And enterprises of great pith and moment

With this regard their currents turn awry

And lose the name of action. Soft you now!

The fair Ophelia! Nymph, in thy orisons

Be all my sins rememb'red.

Ophelia: Good my lord,

How does your honour for this many a day?

Hamlet: I humbly thank you; well, well, well.

Ophelia: My lord, I have remembrances of yours

That I have longed long to re-deliver.

I pray you, now receive them.

Hamlet: No, not I!

I never gave you aught.

Ophelia: My honour'd lord, you know right well you did,

And with them words of so sweet breath compos'd

As made the things more rich. Their perfume lost,

Take these again; for to the noble mind

Rich gifts wax poor when givers prove unkind.

There, my lord.

Hamlet: Ha, ha! Are you honest?

Ophelia: My lord?

Hamlet: Are you fair?

Ophelia: What means your lordship?

Hamlet: That if you be honest and fair, your

honesty should admit no

discourse to your beauty.

Ophelia: Could beauty, my lord, have better commerce than with honesty?

Hamlet: Ay, truly; for the power of beauty will sooner transform honesty from what it is to a bawd than the force of honesty can translate beauty into his likeness. This was sometime a paradox, but now the time gives it proof. I did love you once.

Ophelia: Indeed, my lord, you made me believe so.

Hamlet: You should not have believ'd me; for virtue cannot so inoculate our old stock but we shall relish of it. I loved you not.

Ophelia: I was the more deceived.

Hamlet: Get thee to a nunnery! Why wouldst thou be a breeder of sinners? I am myself indifferent honest, but yet I could accuse me of such things that it were better my mother had not borne me. I am very proud, revengeful, ambitious; with more offences at my beck than I have thoughts to put them in, imagination to give them shape, or time to act them in. What should such fellows as I do, crawling between earth and heaven? We are arrant knaves all; believe none of us. Go thy ways to a nunnery. Where's your father?

Ophelia: At home, my lord.

Hamlet: Let the doors be shut upon him, that he may play the fool nowhere but in's own house. Farewell.

Ophelia: O, help him, you sweet heavens!

Hamlet: If thou dost marry, I'll give thee this plague for thy dowry: be thou as chaste as ice, as pure as snow, thou shalt not escape calumny. Get thee to a nunnery. Go, farewell. Or if thou wilt needs marry, marry a fool; for wise men know well enough what monsters you make of them. To a nunnery, go; and quickly too. Farewell.

Ophelia: O heavenly powers, restore him!

Hamlet: I have heard of your paintings too, well enough. God hath given you one face, and you make yourselves another. You jig, you amble, and you lisp; you nickname God's creatures and make your

wantonness your ignorance. Go to, I'll no more

on't! it hath made me mad. I say, we will have no more marriages. Those that are married already- all but one- shall live; the rest shall keep as they are. To a nunnery, go.
[Exit.]

Ophelia: O, what a noble mind is here o'erthrown!
The courtier's, scholar's, soldier's, eye, tongue, sword,
Th' expectancy and rose of the fair state,
The glass of fashion and the mould of form,
Th' observ'd of all observers- quite, quite down!
And I, of ladies most deject and wretched,
That suck'd the honey of his music vows,
Now see that noble and most sovereign reason,
Like sweet bells jangled, out of tune and harsh;
That unmatch'd form and feature of blown youth
Blasted with ecstasy. O, woe is me
T' have seen what I have seen, see what I see!
[Enter King and Polonius.]

King: Love? his affections do not that way tend;
Nor what he spake, though it lack'd form a little,
Was not like madness. There's something in his soul

O'er which his melancholy sits on brood;

And I do doubt the hatch and the disclose

Will be some danger; which for to prevent,

I have in quick determination

Thus set it down: he shall with speed to England

For the demand of our neglected tribute.

Haply the seas, and countries different,

With variable objects, shall expel

This something-settled matter in his heart,

Whereon his brains still beating puts him thus

From fashion of himself. What think you on't?

Polonius: It shall do well. But yet do I believe

The origin and commencement of his grief

Sprung from neglected love.- How now, Ophelia?

You need not tell us what Lord Hamlet said.

We heard it all.- My lord, do as you please;

But if you hold it fit, after the play

Let his queen mother all alone entreat him

To show his grief. Let her be round with him;

And I'll be plac'd so please you, in the ear

Of all their conference. If she find him not,

To England send him; or confine him where

Your wisdom best shall think.

King: It shall be so.

Madness in great ones must not unwatch'd go.
[Exeunt.]

Scene II - Elsinore. hall in the Castle.

[Enter Hamlet and three of the Players.]

Hamlet: Speak the speech, I pray you, as I pronounc'd it to you, trippingly on the tongue. But if you mouth it, as many of our players do, I had as live the town crier spoke my lines. Nor do not saw the air too much with your hand, thus, but use all gently; for in the very torrent, tempest, and (as I may say) whirlwind of your passion, you must acquire and beget a temperance that may give it smoothness. O, it offends me to the soul to hear a robustious periwig-pated fellow tear a passion to tatters, to very rags, to split the ears of the groundlings, who (for the most part) are capable of nothing but inexplicable dumb shows and noise. I would have such a fellow whipp'd for o'erdoing Termagant. It out-herods Herod. Pray you avoid it.

First Player: I warrant your honour.

Hamlet: Be not too tame neither; but let your

own discretion be your tutor. Suit the action to the word, the word to the action; with this special observance, that you o'erstep not the modesty of nature: for anything so overdone is from the purpose of playing, whose end, both at the first and now, was and is, to hold, as 'twere, the mirror up to nature; to show Virtue her own feature, scorn her own image, and the very age and body of the time his form and pressure. Now this overdone, or come tardy off, though it make the unskilful laugh, cannot but make the judicious grieve; the censure of the which one must in your allowance o'erweigh a whole theatre of others. O, there be players that I have seen play, and heard others praise, and that highly (not to speak it profanely), that, neither having the accent of Christians, nor the gait of Christian, pagan, nor man, have so strutted and bellowed that I have thought some of Nature's journeymen had made men, and not made them well, they imitated humanity so abominably.

First Player: I hope we have reform'd that indifferently with us, sir.

Hamlet: O, reform it altogether! And let those

that play you clowns speak no more than is set down for them. For there be of them that will themselves laugh, to set on some quantity of barren spectators to laugh too, though in the mean time some necessary question of the play be then to be considered. That's villainous and shows a most pitiful ambition in the fool that uses it. Go make you ready.

[Exeunt Players.]

[Enter Polonius, Rosencrantz, and Guildenstern.]

How now, my lord? Will the King hear this piece of work?

Polonius: And the Queen too, and that presently.

Hamlet: Bid the players make haste, [Exit Polonius.] Will you two help to hasten them?

Both: We will, my lord.

[Exeunt they two.]

Hamlet: What, ho, Horatio!

[Enter Horatio.]

Horatio: Here, sweet lord, at your service.

Hamlet: Horatio, thou art e'en as just a man As e'er my conversation cop'd withal.

Horatio: O, my dear lord!

Hamlet: Nay, do not think I flatter;

For what advancement may I hope from thee,

That no revenue hast but thy good spirits

To feed and clothe thee? Why should the poor

be flatter'd?

No, let the candied tongue lick absurd pomp,

And crook the pregnant hinges of the knee

Where thrift may follow fawning. Dost thou hear?

Since my dear soul was mistress of her choice

And could of men distinguish, her election

Hath scald thee for herself. For thou hast been

As one, in suff'ring all, that suffers nothing;

A man that Fortune's buffets and rewards

Hast ta'en with equal thanks; and blest are those

Whose blood and judgment are so well

commingled

That they are not a pipe for Fortune's finger

To sound what stop she please. Give me that

man

That is not passion's slave, and I will wear him

In my heart's core, ay, in my heart of heart,

As I do thee. Something too much of this

There is a play to-night before the King.

One scene of it comes near the circumstance,

Which I have told thee, of my father's death.

I prithee, when thou seest that act afoot,

Even with the very comment of thy soul

Observe my uncle. If his occulted guilt

Do not itself unkennel in one speech,

It is a damned ghost that we have seen,

And my imaginations are as foul

As Vulcan's stithy. Give him heedful note;

For I mine eyes will rivet to his face,

And after we will both our judgments join

In censure of his seeming.

Horatio: Well, my lord.

If he steal aught the whilst this play is playing,

And scape detecting, I will pay the theft.

[Enter Trumpets and Kettledrums. Danish march.

Enter King, Queen, Polonius, Ophelia,

Rosencrantz, Guildenstern, and other Courtiers.]

Hamlet: They are coming to the play. I must be
idle.

Get you a place.

King: How fares our cousin Hamlet?

Hamlet: Excellent, i' faith; of the chameleon's
dish. I eat the air, promise-cramm'd. You cannot

feed capons so.

King: I have nothing with this answer, Hamlet. These words are not mine.

Hamlet: No, nor mine now. [To Polonius] My lord, you play'd once i' th' university, you say?

Polonius: That did I, my lord, and was accounted a good actor.

Hamlet: What did you enact?

Polonius: I did enact Julius Caesar; I was kill'd i' th' Capitol; Brutus kill'd me.

Hamlet: It was a brute part of him to kill so capital a calf there. Be the players ready.

Rosencrantz: Ay, my lord. They stay upon your patience.

Queen: Come hither, my dear Hamlet, sit by me.

Hamlet: No, good mother. Here's metal more attractive.

Polonius: [to the King] O, ho! do you mark that?

Hamlet: Lady, shall I lie in your lap?

[Sits down at Ophelia's feet.]

Ophelia: No, my lord.

Hamlet: I mean, my head upon your lap?

Ophelia: Ay, my lord.

Hamlet: Do you think I meant country matters?

Ophelia: I think nothing, my lord.

Hamlet: That's a fair thought to lie between maids' legs.

Ophelia: What is, my lord?

Hamlet: Nothing.

Ophelia: You are merry, my lord.

Hamlet: Who, I?

Ophelia: Ay, my lord.

Hamlet: O God, your only jig-maker! What should a man do but be merry? For look you how cheerfully my mother looks, and my father died within 's two hours.

Ophelia: Nay 'tis twice two months, my lord.

Hamlet: So long? Nay then, let the devil wear black, for I'll have a suit of sables. O heavens! die two months ago, and not forgotten yet? Then there's hope a great man's memory may outlive his life half a year. But, by'r Lady, he must build churches then; or else shall he suffer not thinking on, with the hobby-horse, whose epitaph is 'For O, for O, the hobby-horse is forgot!'

[Trumpets sound. The dumb show enters.]

Enter a King and a Queen very lovingly; the Queen embracing him and he her. She kneels, and makes show of protestation unto him. He takes her up, and declines his head upon her neck. He lays him down upon a bank of flowers. She, seeing him asleep, leaves him. Anon comes in a fellow, takes off his crown, kisses it, pours poison in the sleeper's ears, and leaves him. The Queen returns, finds the King dead, and makes passionate action. The Poisoner with some three or four Mutes, comes in again, seem to condole with her. The dead body is carried away. The Poisoner wooes the Queen with gifts; she seems harsh and unwilling awhile, but in the end accepts his love.

[Exeunt.]

Ophelia: What means this, my lord?

Hamlet: Marry, this is miching malhecho; it means mischief.

Ophelia: Belike this show imports the argument of the play.

[Enter Prologue.]

Hamlet: We shall know by this fellow. The players cannot keep counsel; they'll tell all.

Ophelia: Will he tell us what this show meant?

Hamlet: Ay, or any show that you'll show him. Be

not you asham'd to show, he'll not shame to tell you what it means.

Ophelia: You are naught, you are naught! I'll mark the play.

Prologue: For us, and for our tragedy,

Here stooping to your clemency,

We beg your hearing patiently.

[Exit.]

Hamlet: Is this a prologue, or the posy of a ring?

Ophelia: 'Tis brief, my lord.

Hamlet: As woman's love.

[Enter two Players as King and Queen.]

  Player King: Full thirty times hath Phoebus' cart gone round

  Neptune's salt wash and Tellus' orbed ground,

  And thirty dozed moons with borrowed sheen

  About the world have times twelve thirties been,

  Since love our hearts, and Hymen did our hands,

  Unite comutual in most sacred bands.

  Player Queen: So many journeys may the sun and moon

  Make us again count o'er ere love be done!

  But woe is me! you are so sick of late,

So far from cheer and from your former state.

That I distrust you. Yet, though I distrust,

Discomfort you, my lord, it nothing must;

For women's fear and love holds quantity,

In neither aught, or in extremity.

Now what my love is, proof hath made you know;

And as my love is siz'd, my fear is so.

Where love is great, the littlest doubts are fear;

Where little fears grow great, great love grows there.

Player King: Faith, I must leave thee, love, and shortly too;

My operant powers their functions leave to do.

And thou shalt live in this fair world behind,

Honour'd, belov'd, and haply one as kind

For husband shalt thou-

Player Queen: O, confound the rest!

Such love must needs be treason in my breast.

When second husband let me be accurst!

None wed the second but who killed the first.

Hamlet: [aside] Wormwood, wormwood!

Player Queen: The instances that second marriage move

Are base respects of thrift, but none of love.

A second time I kill my husband dead

When second husband kisses me in bed.

Player King: I do believe you think what now

you speak;

But what we do determine oft we break.

Purpose is but the slave to memory,

Of violent birth, but poor validity;

Which now, like fruit unripe, sticks on the tree,

But fill unshaken when they mellow be.

Most necessary 'tis that we forget

To pay ourselves what to ourselves is debt.

What to ourselves in passion we propose,

The passion ending, doth the purpose lose.

The violence of either grief or joy

Their own enactures with themselves destroy.

Where joy most revels, grief doth most lament;

Grief joys, joy grieves, on slender accident.

This world is not for aye, nor 'tis not strange

That even our loves should with our fortunes

change;

For 'tis a question left us yet to prove,

Whether love lead fortune, or else fortune love.

The great man down, you mark his favourite

flies,

The poor advanc'd makes friends of enemies;

And hitherto doth love on fortune tend,

For who not needs shall never lack a friend,

And who in want a hollow friend doth try,

Directly seasons him his enemy.

But, orderly to end where I begun,

Our wills and fates do so contrary run

That our devices still are overthrown;

Our thoughts are ours, their ends none of our own.

So think thou wilt no second husband wed;

But die thy thoughts when thy first lord is dead.

Player Queen: Nor earth to me give food, nor heaven light,

Sport and repose lock from me day and night,

To desperation turn my trust and hope,

An anchor's cheer in prison be my scope,

Each opposite that blanks the face of joy

Meet what I would have well, and it destroy,

Both here and hence pursue me lasting strife,

If, once a widow, ever I be wife!

Hamlet: If she should break it now!

Player King: 'Tis deeply sworn. Sweet, leave

me here awhile.

My spirits grow dull, and fain I would beguile

The tedious day with sleep.

Player Queen: Sleep rock thy brain,

[He sleeps.]

And never come mischance between us twain!

[Exit.]

Hamlet: Madam, how like you this play?

Queen: The lady doth protest too much, methinks.

Hamlet: O, but she'll keep her word.

King: Have you heard the argument? Is there no offence in't?

Hamlet: No, no! They do but jest, poison in jest; no offence i' th' world.

King: What do you call the play?

Hamlet: 'The Mousetrap.' Marry, how? Tropically. This play is the image of a murder done in Vienna. Gonzago is the duke's name; his wife, Baptista. You shall see anon. 'Tis a knavish piece of work; but what o' that? Your Majesty, and we that have free souls, it touches us not. Let the gall'd jade winch; our withers are unwrung.

[Enter Lucianus.]

This is one Lucianus, nephew to the King.

Ophelia: You are as good as a chorus, my lord.

Hamlet: I could interpret between you and your love, if I could see the puppets dallying.

Ophelia: You are keen, my lord, you are keen.

Hamlet: It would cost you a groaning to take off my edge.

Ophelia: Still better, and worse.

Hamlet: So you must take your husbands.- Begin, murderer. Pox, leave thy damnable faces, and begin! Come, the croaking raven doth bellow for revenge.

Lucianus: Thoughts black, hands apt, drugs fit, and time agreeing;

Confederate season, else no creature seeing;

Thou mixture rank, of midnight weeds collected,

With Hecate's ban thrice blasted, thrice infected,

Thy natural magic and dire property

On wholesome life usurp immediately.

Pours the poison in his ears.

Hamlet: He poisons him i' th' garden for's estate. His name's Gonzago. The story is extant, and written in very choice Italian. You shall see anon how the murderer gets the love of Gonzago's wife.

Ophelia: The King rises.

Hamlet: What, frighted with false fire?

Queen: How fares my lord?

Polonius: Give o'er the play.

King: Give me some light! Away!

All: Lights, lights, lights!

[Exeunt all but Hamlet and Horatio.]

Hamlet: Why, let the strucken deer go weep,

The hart ungalled play;

For some must watch, while some must sleep:

Thus runs the world away.

Would not this, sir, and a forest of feathers- if the rest of my

fortunes turn Turk with me-with two Provincial roses on my raz'd

shoes, get me a fellowship in a cry of players, sir?

Horatio: Half a share.

Hamlet: A whole one I!

For thou dost know, O Damon dear,

This realm dismantled was

Of Jove himself; and now reigns here

A very, very- pajock.

Horatio: You might have rhym'd.

Hamlet: O good Horatio, I'll take the ghost's word for a thousand
pound! Didst perceive?

Horatio: Very well, my lord.

Hamlet: Upon the talk of the poisoning?

Horatio: I did very well note him.

Hamlet: Aha! Come, some music! Come, the recorders!
For if the King like not the comedy,
Why then, belike he likes it not, perdy.
Come, some music!

[Enter Rosencrantz and Guildenstern.]

Guildenstern: Good my lord, vouchsafe me a word with you.

Hamlet: Sir, a whole history.

Guildenstern: The King, sir-

Hamlet: Ay, sir, what of him?

Guildenstern: Is in his retirement, marvellous distemper'd.

Hamlet: With drink, sir?

Guildenstern: No, my lord; rather with choler.

Hamlet: Your wisdom should show itself more

richer to signify this to the doctor; for me to put him to his purgation would perhaps plunge him into far more choler.

Guildenstern: Good my lord, put your discourse into some frame, and start not so wildly from my affair.

Hamlet: I am tame, sir; pronounce.

Guildenstern: The Queen, your mother, in most great affliction of spirit hath sent me to you.

Hamlet: You are welcome.

Guildenstern: Nay, good my lord, this courtesy is not of the right breed. If it shall please you to make me a wholesome answer, I will do your mother's commandment; if not, your pardon and my return shall be the end of my business.

Hamlet: Sir, I cannot.

Guildenstern: What, my lord?

Hamlet: Make you a wholesome answer; my wit's diseas'd. But, sir, such answer is I can make, you shall command; or rather, as you say, my mother. Therefore no more, but to the matter! My mother, you say-

Rosencrantz: Then thus she says: your behaviour hath struck her into amazement and admiration.

Hamlet: O wonderful son, that can so stonish a mother! But is there no sequel at the heels of this mother's admiration? Impart.

Rosencrantz: She desires to speak with you in her closet ere you go to bed.

Hamlet: We shall obey, were she ten times our mother. Have you any further trade with us?

Rosencrantz: My lord, you once did love me.

Hamlet: And do still, by these pickers and stealers!

Rosencrantz: Good my lord, what is your cause of distemper? You do surely bar the door upon your own liberty, if you deny your griefs to your friend.

Hamlet: Sir, I lack advancement.

Rosencrantz: How can that be, when you have the voice of the King himself for your succession in Denmark?

Hamlet: Ay, sir, but 'while the grass grows'- the proverb is something musty.

[Enter the Players with recorders.]

O, the recorders! Let me see one. To withdraw with you- why do you go about to recover the wind of me, as if you would drive me into a toil?

Guildenstern: O my lord, if my duty be too bold, my love is too unmannerly.

Hamlet: I do not well understand that. Will you play upon this pipe?

Guildenstern: My lord, I cannot.

Hamlet: I pray you.

Guildenstern: Believe me, I cannot.

Hamlet: I do beseech you.

Guildenstern: I know, no touch of it, my lord.

Hamlet: It is as easy as lying. Govern these ventages with your fingers and thumbs, give it breath with your mouth, and it will discourse most eloquent music. Look you, these are the stops.

Guildenstern: But these cannot I command to any utt'rance of harmony. I have not the skill.

Hamlet: Why, look you now, how unworthy a thing you make of me! You would play upon me; you would seem to know my stops; you would pluck out the heart of my mystery; you would sound me from my lowest note to the top of my compass; and there is much music, excellent voice, in this little organ, yet cannot you make it speak. 'Sblood, do you think I am easier to be play'd on than a pipe? Call me what instrument you will, though you can fret me, you cannot play upon me.

[Enter Polonius.]

God bless you, sir!

Polonius: My lord, the Queen would speak with you, and presently.

Hamlet: Do you see yonder cloud that's almost in shape of a camel?

Polonius: By th' mass, and 'tis like a camel indeed.

Hamlet: Methinks it is like a weasel.

Polonius: It is back'd like a weasel.

Hamlet: Or like a whale.

Polonius: Very like a whale.

Hamlet: Then will I come to my mother by-and-by.- They fool me to the

top of my bent.- I will come by-and-by.

Polonius: I will say so.

[Exit.]

Hamlet: 'By-and-by' is easily said.- Leave me, friends.

[Exeunt all but Hamlet.]

'Tis now the very witching time of night,

When churchyards yawn, and hell itself breathes out

Contagion to this world. Now could I drink hot blood

And do such bitter business as the day

Would quake to look on. Soft! now to my mother!

O heart, lose not thy nature; let not ever

The soul of Nero enter this firm bosom.

Let me be cruel, not unnatural;

I will speak daggers to her, but use none.

My tongue and soul in this be hypocrites-

How in my words somever she be shent,

To give them seals never, my soul, consent!

[Exit.]

Scene III - A room in the Castle.

[Enter King, Rosencrantz, and Guildenstern.]

King: I like him not, nor stands it safe with us

To let his madness range. Therefore prepare you;

I your commission will forthwith dispatch,

And he to England shall along with you.

The terms of our estate may not endure

Hazard so near us as doth hourly grow

Out of his lunacies.

Guildenstern: We will ourselves provide.

Most holy and religious fear it is

To keep those many many bodies safe

That live and feed upon your Majesty.

Rosencrantz: The single and peculiar life is bound

With all the strength and armour of the mind

To keep itself from noyance; but much more

That spirit upon whose weal depends and rests

The lives of many. The cess of majesty

Dies not alone, but like a gulf doth draw

What's near it with it. It is a massy wheel,

Fix'd on the summit of the highest mount,

To whose huge spokes ten thousand lesser things

Are mortis'd and adjoin'd; which when it falls,

Each small annexment, petty consequence,

Attends the boist'rous ruin. Never alone

Did the king sigh, but with a general groan.

King: Arm you, I pray you, to th', speedy voyage;

For we will fetters put upon this fear,

Which now goes too free-footed.

Both: We will haste us.

[Exeunt Gentlemen.]

[Enter Polonius.]

Polonius: My lord, he's going to his mother's closet.

Behind the arras I'll convey myself

To hear the process. I'll warrant she'll tax him home;

And, as you said, and wisely was it said,

'Tis meet that some more audience than a mother,

Since nature makes them partial, should o'erhear

The speech, of vantage. Fare you well, my liege.

I'll call upon you ere you go to bed

And tell you what I know.

King: Thanks, dear my lord.

[Exit Polonius.]

O, my offence is rank, it smells to heaven;

It hath the primal eldest curse upon't,

A brother's murder! Pray can I not,

Though inclination be as sharp as will.

My stronger guilt defeats my strong intent,

And, like a man to double business bound,

I stand in pause where I shall first begin,

And both neglect. What if this cursed hand

Were thicker than itself with brother's blood,

Is there not rain enough in the sweet heavens

To wash it white as snow? Whereto serves

mercy

But to confront the visage of offence?

And what's in prayer but this twofold force,

To be forestalled ere we come to fall,

Or pardon'd being down? Then I'll look up;

My fault is past. But, O, what form of prayer

Can serve my turn? 'Forgive me my foul

murder'?

That cannot be; since I am still possess'd

Of those effects for which I did the murder-

My crown, mine own ambition, and my Queen.

May one be pardon'd and retain th' offence?

In the corrupted currents of this world

Offence's gilded hand may shove by justice,

And oft 'tis seen the wicked prize itself

Buys out the law; but 'tis not so above.

There is no shuffling; there the action lies

In his true nature, and we ourselves compell'd,

Even to the teeth and forehead of our faults,

To give in evidence. What then? What rests?

Try what repentance can. What can it not?

Yet what can it when one cannot repent?

O wretched state! O bosom black as death!

O limed soul, that, struggling to be free,

Art more engag'd! Help, angels! Make assay.

Bow, stubborn knees; and heart with strings of
steel,

Be soft as sinews of the new-born babe!

All may be well.   [He kneels.]

[Enter Hamlet.]

Hamlet: Now might I do it pat, now he is praying;

And now I'll do't. [He draws his sword.] And so
he goes to heaven,

And so am I reveng'd. That would be scann'd.

A villain kills my father; and for that,

I, his sole son, do this same villain send

To heaven.

Why, this is hire and salary, not revenge!

He took my father grossly, full of bread,

With all his crimes broad blown, as flush as May;

And how his audit stands, who knows save
heaven?

But in our circumstance and course of thought,

'Tis heavy with him; and am I then reveng'd,

To take him in the purging of his soul,

When he is fit and seasoned for his passage?

No. [He sheaths his sword.]

Up, sword, and know thou a more horrid hent.

When he is drunk asleep; or in his rage;

Or in th' incestuous pleasure of his bed;

At gaming, swearing, or about some act

That has no relish of salvation in't-

Then trip him, that his heels may kick at heaven,

And that his soul may be as damn'd and black

As hell, whereto it goes. My mother stays.

This physic but prolongs thy sickly days.

[Exit.]

King: [rises] My words fly up, my thoughts remain below.

Words without thoughts never to heaven go.

[Exit.]

Scene IV - The Queen's closet.

[Enter Queen and Polonius.]

Polonius: He will come straight. Look you lay home to him.

Tell him his pranks have been too broad to bear with,

And that your Grace hath screen'd and stood between

Much heat and him. I'll silence me even here.

Pray you be round with him.

Hamlet: [within] Mother, mother, mother!

Queen: I'll warrant you; fear me not. Withdraw; I hear him coming.

[Polonius hides behind the arras.]

[Enter Hamlet.]

Hamlet: Now, mother, what's the matter?

Queen: Hamlet, thou hast thy father much offended.

Hamlet: Mother, you have my father much offended.

Queen: Come, come, you answer with an idle tongue.

Hamlet: Go, go, you question with a wicked tongue.

Queen: Why, how now, Hamlet?

Hamlet: What's the matter now?

Queen: Have you forgot me?

Hamlet: No, by the rood, not so!

You are the Queen, your husband's brother's wife,

And (would it were not so!) you are my mother.

Queen: Nay, then I'll set those to you that can speak.

Hamlet: Come, come, and sit you down. You shall not budge I

You go not till I set you up a glass

Where you may see the inmost part of you.

Queen: What wilt thou do? Thou wilt not murder me?

Help, help, ho!

Polonius: [behind] What, ho! help, help, help!

Hamlet: [draws] How now? a rat? Dead for a ducat, dead!

[Makes a pass through the arras and kills Polonius.]

Polonius: [behind] O, I am slain!

Queen: O me, what hast thou done?

Hamlet: Nay, I know not. Is it the King?

Queen: O, what a rash and bloody deed is this!

Hamlet: A bloody deed- almost as bad, good mother,

As kill a king, and marry with his brother.

Queen: As kill a king?

Hamlet: Ay, lady, it was my word.

[Lifts up the arras and sees Polonius.]

Thou wretched, rash, intruding fool, farewell!

I took thee for thy better. Take thy fortune.

Thou find'st to be too busy is some danger.

Leave wringing of your hinds. Peace! sit you down

And let me wring your heart; for so I shall

If it be made of penetrable stuff;

If damned custom have not braz'd it so

That it is proof and bulwark against sense.

Queen: What have I done that thou dar'st wag thy tongue

In noise so rude against me?

Hamlet: Such an act

That blurs the grace and blush of modesty;

Calls virtue hypocrite; takes off the rose

From the fair forehead of an innocent love,

And sets a blister there; makes marriage vows

As false as dicers' oaths. O, such a deed

As from the body of contraction plucks

The very soul, and sweet religion makes

A rhapsody of words! Heaven's face doth glow;

Yea, this solidity and compound mass,

With tristful visage, as against the doom,

Is thought-sick at the act.

Queen: Ay me, what act,

That roars so loud and thunders in the index?

Hamlet: Look here upon th's picture, and on this,

The counterfeit presentment of two brothers.

See what a grace was seated on this brow;

Hyperion's curls; the front of Jove himself;

An eye like Mars, to threaten and command;

A station like the herald Mercury

New lighted on a heaven-kissing hill:

A combination and a form indeed

Where every god did seem to set his seal

To give the world assurance of a man.

This was your husband. Look you now what

follows.

Here is your husband, like a mildew'd ear

Blasting his wholesome brother. Have you eyes?

Could you on this fair mountain leave to feed,

And batten on this moor? Ha! have you eyes

You cannot call it love; for at your age

The heyday in the blood is tame, it's humble,

And waits upon the judgment; and what

judgment

Would step from this to this? Sense sure you have,

Else could you not have motion; but sure that sense

Is apoplex'd; for madness would not err,

Nor sense to ecstacy was ne'er so thrall'd

But it reserv'd some quantity of choice

To serve in such a difference. What devil was't

That thus hath cozen'd you at hoodman-blind?

Eyes without feeling, feeling without sight,

Ears without hands or eyes, smelling sans all,

Or but a sickly part of one true sense

Could not so mope.

O shame! where is thy blush? Rebellious hell,

If thou canst mutine in a matron's bones,

To flaming youth let virtue be as wax

And melt in her own fire. Proclaim no shame

When the compulsive ardour gives the charge,

Since frost itself as actively doth burn,

And reason panders will.

Queen: O Hamlet, speak no more!

Thou turn'st mine eyes into my very soul,

And there I see such black and grained spots

As will not leave their tinct.

Hamlet: Nay, but to live

In the rank sweat of an enseamed bed,

Stew'd in corruption, honeying and making love

Over the nasty sty!

Queen: O, speak to me no more!

These words like daggers enter in mine ears.

No more, sweet Hamlet!

Hamlet: A murderer and a villain!

A slave that is not twentieth part the tithe

Of your precedent lord; a vice of kings;

A cutpurse of the empire and the rule,

That from a shelf the precious diadem stole

And put it in his pocket!

Queen: No more!

[Enter the Ghost in his nightgown.]

Hamlet: A king of shreds and patches!-

Save me and hover o'er me with your wings,

You heavenly guards! What would your gracious

figure?

Queen: Alas, he's mad!

Hamlet: Do you not come your tardy son to

chide,

That, laps'd in time and passion, lets go by

Th' important acting of your dread command?

O, say!

Ghost: Do not forget. This visitation

Is but to whet thy almost blunted purpose.

But look, amazement on thy mother sits.

O, step between her and her fighting soul

Conceit in weakest bodies strongest works.

Speak to her, Hamlet.

Hamlet: How is it with you, lady?

Queen: Alas, how is't with you,

That you do bend your eye on vacancy,

And with th' encorporal air do hold discourse?

Forth at your eyes your spirits wildly peep;

And, as the sleeping soldiers in th' alarm,

Your bedded hairs, like life in excrements,

Start up and stand an end. O gentle son,

Upon the beat and flame of thy distemper

Sprinkle cool patience! Whereon do you look?

Hamlet: On him, on him! Look you how pale he glares!

His form and cause conjoin'd, preaching to stones,

Would make them capable.- Do not look upon me,

Lest with this piteous action you convert

My stern effects. Then what I have to do

Will want true colour- tears perchance for blood.

Queen: To whom do you speak this?

Hamlet: Do you see nothing there?

Queen: Nothing at all; yet all that is I see.

Hamlet: Nor did you nothing hear?

Queen: No, nothing but ourselves.

Hamlet: Why, look you there! Look how it steals away!

My father, in his habit as he liv'd!

Look where he goes even now out at the portal!

[Exit Ghost.]

Queen: This is the very coinage of your brain.

This bodiless creation ecstasy

Is very cunning in.

Hamlet: Ecstasy?

My pulse as yours doth temperately keep time

And makes as healthful music. It is not madness

That I have utt'red. Bring me to the test,

And I the matter will reword; which madness

Would gambol from. Mother, for love of grace,

Lay not that flattering unction to your soul

That not your trespass but my madness speaks.

It will but skin and film the ulcerous place,

Whiles rank corruption, mining all within,

Infects unseen. Confess yourself to heaven;

Repent what's past; avoid what is to come;

And do not spread the compost on the weeds

To make them ranker. Forgive me this my virtue;

For in the fatness of these pursy times

Virtue itself of vice must pardon beg-

Yea, curb and woo for leave to do him good.

Queen: O Hamlet, thou hast cleft my heart in twain.

Hamlet: O, throw away the worser part of it,

And live the purer with the other half,

Good night- but go not to my uncle's bed.

Assume a virtue, if you have it not.

That monster, custom, who all sense doth eat

Of habits evil, is angel yet in this,

That to the use of actions fair and good

He likewise gives a frock or livery,

That aptly is put on. Refrain to-night,

And that shall lend a kind of easiness

To the next abstinence; the next more easy;

For use almost can change the stamp of nature,

And either serve the devil, or throw him out

With wondrous potency. Once more, good night;

And when you are desirous to be blest,

I'll blessing beg of you.- For this same lord,

I do repent; but heaven hath pleas'd it so,

To punish me with this, and this with me,

That I must be their scourge and minister.

I will bestow him, and will answer well

The death I gave him. So again, good night.

I must be cruel, only to be kind;

Thus bad begins, and worse remains behind.

One word more, good lady.

Queen: What shall I do?

Hamlet: Not this, by no means, that I bid you do:

Let the bloat King tempt you again to bed;

Pinch wanton on your cheek; call you his mouse;

And let him, for a pair of reechy kisses,

Or paddling in your neck with his damn'd fingers,

Make you to ravel all this matter out,

That I essentially am not in madness,

But mad in craft. 'Twere good you let him know;

For who that's but a queen, fair, sober, wise,

Would from a paddock, from a bat, a gib

Such dear concernings hide? Who would do so?

No, in despite of sense and secrecy,

Unpeg the basket on the house's top,

Let the birds fly, and like the famous ape,

To try conclusions, in the basket creep

And break your own neck down.

Queen: Be thou assur'd, if words be made of breath,

And breath of life, I have no life to breathe

What thou hast said to me.

Hamlet: I must to England; you know that?

Queen: Alack,

I had forgot! 'Tis so concluded on.

Hamlet: There's letters seal'd; and my two schoolfellows,

Whom I will trust as I will adders fang'd,

They bear the mandate; they must sweep my way

And marshal me to knavery. Let it work;

For 'tis the sport to have the enginer

Hoist with his own petar; and 't shall go hard

But I will delve one yard below their mines

And blow them at the moon. O, 'tis most sweet

When in one line two crafts directly meet.

This man shall set me packing.

I'll lug the guts into the neighbour room.-

Mother, good night.- Indeed, this counsellor

Is now most still, most secret, and most grave,

Who was in life a foolish peating knave.

Come, sir, to draw toward an end with you.

Good night, mother.

[Exit Hamlet, tugging Polonius.]

My Notes

ACT IV

Scene I - Elsinore. A room in the Castle.

[Enter King and Queen, with Rosencrantz and Guildenstern.]

King: There's matter in these sighs. These profound heaves
You must translate; 'tis fit we understand them.
Where is your son?

Queen: Bestow this place on us a little while.

[Exeunt Rosencrantz and Guildenstern.]

Ah, mine own lord, what have I seen to-night!

King: What, Gertrude? How does Hamlet?

Queen: Mad as the sea and wind when both contend
Which is the mightier. In his lawless fit
Behind the arras hearing something stir,
Whips out his rapier, cries 'A rat, a rat!'
And in this brainish apprehension kills
The unseen good old man.

King: O heavy deed!
It had been so with us, had we been there.
His liberty is full of threats to all-

To you yourself, to us, to every one.

Alas, how shall this bloody deed be answer'd?

It will be laid to us, whose providence

Should have kept short, restrain'd, and out of
haunt

This mad young man. But so much was our love

We would not understand what was most fit,

But, like the owner of a foul disease,

To keep it from divulging, let it feed

Even on the pith of life. Where is he gone?

Queen: To draw apart the body he hath kill'd;

O'er whom his very madness, like some ore

Among a mineral of metals base,

Shows itself pure. He weeps for what is done.

King: O Gertrude, come away!

The sun no sooner shall the mountains touch

But we will ship him hence; and this vile deed

We must with all our majesty and skill

Both countenance and excuse. Ho, Guildenstern!

[Enter Rosencrantz and Guildenstern.]

Friends both, go join you with some further aid.

Hamlet in madness hath Polonius slain,

And from his mother's closet hath he dragg'd
him.

Go seek him out; speak fair, and bring the body

Into the chapel. I pray you haste in this.

[Exeunt Rosencrantz and Guildenstern.]

Come, Gertrude, we'll call up our wisest friends

And let them know both what we mean to do

And what's untimely done. [So haply slander,]

Whose whisper o'er the world's diameter,

As level as the cannon to his blank,

Transports his poisoned shot- may miss our name

And hit the woundless air.- O, come away!

My soul is full of discord and dismay.

[Exeunt.]

Scene II - Elsinore. A room in the Castle.

[Enter Hamlet.]

Hamlet: Safely stow'd.

Calling Without: Hamlet! Lord Hamlet!

Hamlet: But soft! What noise? Who calls on Hamlet? O, here they come.

[Enter Rosencrantz and Guildenstern.]

Rosencrantz: What have you done, my lord, with the dead body?

Hamlet: Compounded it with dust, whereto 'tis kin.

Rosencrantz: Tell us where 'tis, that we may take it thence
And bear it to the chapel.

Hamlet: Do not believe it.

Rosencrantz: Believe what?

Hamlet: That I can keep your counsel, and not mine own. Besides, to be
demanded of a sponge, what replication should be made by the son of a king?

Rosencrantz: Take you me for a sponge, my lord?

Hamlet: Ay, sir; that soaks up the King's countenance, his rewards, his authorities. But such officers do the King best service in the end. He keeps them, like an ape, in the corner of his jaw; first mouth'd, to be last swallowed. When he needs what you have glean'd, it is but squeezing you and, sponge, you shall be dry again.

Rosencrantz: I understand you not, my lord.

Hamlet: I am glad of it. A knavish speech sleeps in a foolish ear.

Rosencrantz: My lord, you must tell us where

the body is and go with us to
the King.

Hamlet: The body is with the King, but the King
is not with the body.
The King is a thing.

Guildenstern: A thing, my lord?

Hamlet: Of nothing. Bring me to him. Hide fox,
and all after.

[Exeunt.]

Scene III - Elsinore. A room in the Castle.

[Enter King.]

King: I have sent to seek him and to find the
body.
How dangerous is it that this man goes loose!
Yet must not we put the strong law on him.
He's lov'd of the distracted multitude,
Who like not in their judgment, but their eyes;
And where 'tis so, th' offender's scourge is
weigh'd,
But never the offence. To bear all smooth and
even,
This sudden sending him away must seem

Deliberate pause. Diseases desperate grown

By desperate appliance are reliev'd,

Or not at all.

[Enter Rosencrantz.]

How now! What hath befall'n?

Rosencrantz: Where the dead body is bestow'd,
my lord,

We cannot get from him.

King: But where is he?

Rosencrantz: Without, my lord; guarded, to
know your pleasure.

King: Bring him before us.

Rosencrantz: Ho, Guildenstern! Bring in my
lord.

[Enter Hamlet and Guildenstern with Attendants].

King: Now, Hamlet, where's Polonius?

Hamlet: At supper.

King: At supper? Where?

Hamlet: Not where he eats, but where he is
eaten. A certain convocation of politic worms are
e'en at him. Your worm is your only emperor for
diet. We fat all creatures else to fat us, and we
fat ourselves for maggots. Your fat king and your
lean beggar is but variable service- two dishes,

but to one table. That's the end.

King: Alas, alas!

Hamlet: A man may fish with the worm that hath eat of a king, and eat of the fish that hath fed of that worm.

King: What dost thou mean by this?

Hamlet: Nothing but to show you how a king may go a progress through the guts of a beggar.

King: Where is Polonius?

Hamlet: In heaven. Send thither to see. If your messenger find him not there, seek him i' th' other place yourself. But indeed, if you find him not within this month, you shall nose him as you go up the stair, into the lobby.

King: [To Attendants] Go seek him there.

Hamlet: He will stay till you come.

[Exeunt Attendants.]

King: Hamlet, this deed, for thine especial safety,-

Which we do tender as we dearly grieve

For that which thou hast done,- must send thee hence

With fiery quickness. Therefore prepare thyself.

The bark is ready and the wind at help,

Th' associates tend, and everything is bent

For England.

Hamlet: For England?

King: Ay, Hamlet.

Hamlet: Good.

King: So is it, if thou knew'st our purposes.

Hamlet: I see a cherub that sees them. But

come, for England!

Farewell, dear mother.

King: Thy loving father, Hamlet.

Hamlet: My mother! Father and mother is man

and wife; man and wife is

one flesh; and so, my mother. Come, for

England!

[Exit.]

King: Follow him at foot; tempt him with speed

aboard.

Delay it not; I'll have him hence to-night.

Away! for everything is seal'd and done

That else leans on th' affair. Pray you make

haste.

[Exeunt Rosencrantz and Guildenstern]

And, England, if my love thou hold'st at aught,-

As my great power thereof may give thee sense,

Since yet thy cicatrice looks raw and red

After the Danish sword, and thy free awe

Pays homage to us,- thou mayst not coldly set

Our sovereign process, which imports at full,

By letters congruing to that effect,

The present death of Hamlet. Do it, England;

For like the hectic in my blood he rages,

And thou must cure me. Till I know 'tis done,

Howe'er my haps, my joys were ne'er begun.

[Exit.]

Scene IV - A plain, near Elsinore.

[Enter Fortinbras with his Army over the stage.]

Fortinbras: Go, Captain, from me greet the

Danish King.

Tell him that by his license Fortinbras

Craves the conveyance of a promis'd march

Over his kingdom. You know the rendezvous.

if that his Majesty would aught with us,

We shall express our duty in his eye;

And let him know so.

Captain: I will do't, my lord.

Fortinbras: Go softly on.

[Exeunt all but the Captain.]

[Enter Hamlet, Rosencrantz, Guildenstern, and others.]

Hamlet: Good sir, whose powers are these?

Captain: They are of Norway, sir.

Hamlet: How purpos'd, sir, I pray you?

Captain: Against some part of Poland.

Hamlet: Who commands them, sir?

Captain: The nephew to old Norway, Fortinbras.

Hamlet: Goes it against the main of Poland, sir,
Or for some frontier?

Captain: Truly to speak, and with no addition,
We go to gain a little patch of ground
That hath in it no profit but the name.
To pay five ducats, five, I would not farm it;
Nor will it yield to Norway or the Pole
A ranker rate, should it be sold in fee.

Hamlet: Why, then the Polack never will defend it.

Captain: Yes, it is already garrison'd.

Hamlet: Two thousand souls and twenty thousand ducats
Will not debate the question of this straw.
This is th' imposthume of much wealth and

peace,

That inward breaks, and shows no cause without

Why the man dies.- I humbly thank you, sir.

Captain: God b' wi' you, sir.

[Exit.]

Rosencrantz: Will't please you go, my lord?

Hamlet: I'll be with you straight. Go a little
before.

[Exeunt all but Hamlet.]

How all occasions do inform against me

And spur my dull revenge! What is a man,

If his chief good and market of his time

Be but to sleep and feed? A beast, no more.

Sure he that made us with such large discourse,

Looking before and after, gave us not

That capability and god-like reason

To fust in us unus'd. Now, whether it be

Bestial oblivion, or some craven scruple

Of thinking too precisely on th' event,-

A thought which, quarter'd, hath but one part
wisdom

And ever three parts coward,- I do not know

Why yet I live to say 'This thing's to do,'

Sith I have cause, and will, and strength, and

means

To do't. Examples gross as earth exhort me.

Witness this army of such mass and charge,

Led by a delicate and tender prince,

Whose spirit, with divine ambition puff'd,

Makes mouths at the invisible event,

Exposing what is mortal and unsure

To all that fortune, death, and danger dare,

Even for an eggshell. Rightly to be great

Is not to stir without great argument,

But greatly to find quarrel in a straw

When honour's at the stake. How stand I then,

That have a father kill'd, a mother stain'd,

Excitements of my reason and my blood,

And let all sleep, while to my shame I see

The imminent death of twenty thousand men

That for a fantasy and trick of fame

Go to their graves like beds, fight for a plot

Whereon the numbers cannot try the cause,

Which is not tomb enough and continent

To hide the slain? O, from this time forth,

My thoughts be bloody, or be nothing worth!

[Exit.]

Scene V - Elsinore. A room in the Castle.

[Enter Horatio, Queen, and a Gentleman.]

Queen: I will not speak with her.

Gentleman: She is importunate, indeed distract.

Her mood will needs be pitied.

Queen: What would she have?

Gentleman: She speaks much of her father;

says she hears

There's tricks i' th' world, and hems, and beats

her heart;

Spurns enviously at straws; speaks things in

doubt,

That carry but half sense. Her speech is nothing,

Yet the unshaped use of it doth move

The hearers to collection; they aim at it,

And botch the words up fit to their own thoughts;

Which, as her winks and nods and gestures yield

them,

Indeed would make one think there might be

thought,

Though nothing sure, yet much unhappily.

Horatio: 'Twere good she were spoken with; for

she may strew

Dangerous conjectures in ill-breeding minds.

Queen: Let her come in.

[Exit Gentleman.]

[Aside] To my sick soul, as sin's true nature is

Each toy seems prologue to some great amiss.

So full of artless jealousy is guilt

It spills itself in fearing to be spilt.

[Enter Ophelia distracted, carrying a lute.]

Ophelia: Where is the beauteous Majesty of Denmark?

Queen: How now, Ophelia?

Ophelia: (Sings)

How should I your true-love know

From another one?

By his cockle bat and' staff

And his sandal shoon.

Queen: Alas, sweet lady, what imports this song?

Ophelia: Say you? Nay, pray You mark.

(Sings) *He is dead and gone, lady,*

He is dead and gone;

At his head a grass-green turf,

At his heels a stone.

O, ho!

Queen: Nay, but Ophelia-

Ophelia: Pray you mark.

(Sings) *White his shroud as the mountain snow-*

[Enter King.]

Queen: Alas, look here, my lord!

Ophelia: (Sings)

Larded all with sweet flowers;

Which bewept to the grave did not go

With true-love showers.

King: How do you, pretty lady?

Ophelia: Well, God dild you! They say the owl was a baker's daughter. Lord, we know what we are, but know not what we may be. God be at your table!

King: Conceit upon her father.

Ophelia: Pray let's have no words of this; but when they ask, you what it means, say you this:

(Sings) *To-morrow is Saint Valentine's day,*

All in the morning bedtime,

And I a maid at your window,

To be your Valentine.

Then up he rose and donn'd his clo'es

And dupp'd the chamber door,

Let in the maid, that out a maid

Never departed more.

King: *Pretty Ophelia!*

Ophelia: *Indeed, la, without an oath, I'll make an*

end on't!

(Sings) *By Gis and by Saint Charity,*

Alack, and fie for shame!

Young men will do't if they come to't

By Cock, they are to blame.

Quoth she, 'Before you tumbled me,

You promis'd me to wed.'

He answers:

> *'So would I 'a' done, by yonder sun,*
>> *An thou hadst not come to my bed.'*

King: How long hath she been thus?

Ophelia: I hope all will be well. We must be patient; but I cannot choose but weep to think they would lay him i' th' cold ground. My brother shall know of it; and so I thank you for your good counsel. Come, my coach! Good night, ladies. Good night, sweet ladies. Good night, good night.

[Exit.]

King: Follow her close; give her good watch, I

pray you.

[Exit Horatio.]

O, this is the poison of deep grief; it springs

All from her father's death. O Gertrude, Gertrude,

When sorrows come, they come not single spies.

But in battalions! First, her father slain;

Next, Your son gone, and he most violent author

Of his own just remove; the people muddied,

Thick and and unwholesome in their thoughts
and whispers

For good Polonius' death, and we have done but
greenly

In hugger-mugger to inter him; Poor Ophelia

Divided from herself and her fair-judgment,

Without the which we are pictures or mere
beasts;

Last, and as such containing as all these,

Her brother is in secret come from France;

And wants not buzzers to infect his ear

Feeds on his wonder, keep, himself in clouds,

With pestilent speeches of his father's death,

Wherein necessity, of matter beggar'd,

Will nothing stick Our person to arraign

In ear and ear. O my dear Gertrude, this,

Like to a murd'ring piece, in many places

Give, me superfluous death.

[A noise within.]

Queen: Alack, what noise is this?

King: Where are my Switzers? Let them guard

the door.

[Enter a Messenger.]

What is the matter?

Messenger: Save Yourself, my lord:

The ocean, overpeering of his list,

Eats not the flats with more impetuous haste

Than young Laertes, in a riotous head,

O'erbears your offices. The rabble call him lord;

And, as the world were now but to begin,

Antiquity forgot, custom not known,

The ratifiers and props of every word,

They cry 'Choose we! Laertes shall be king!'

Caps, hands, and tongues applaud it to the

clouds,

'Laertes shall be king! Laertes king!'

[A noise within.]

Queen: How cheerfully on the false trail they cry!

O, this is counter, you false Danish dogs!

King: The doors are broke.

[Enter Laertes with others.]

Laertes: Where is this king?- Sirs, staid you all without.

All: No, let's come in!

Laertes: I pray you give me leave.

All: We will, we will!

Laertes: I thank you. Keep the door.

[Exeunt his Followers.]

O thou vile king,

Give me my father!

Queen: Calmly, good Laertes.

Laertes: That drop of blood that's calm proclaims me bastard;

Cries cuckold to my father; brands the harlot

Even here between the chaste unsmirched brows

Of my true mother.

King: What is the cause, Laertes,

That thy rebellion looks so giant-like?

Let him go, Gertrude. Do not fear our person.

There's such divinity doth hedge a king

That treason can but peep to what it would,

Acts little of his will. Tell me, Laertes,

Why thou art thus incens'd. Let him go, Gertrude.

Speak, man.

Laertes: Where is my father?

King: Dead.

Queen: But not by him!

King: Let him demand his fill.

Laertes: How came he dead? I'll not be juggled with:

To hell, allegiance! vows, to the blackest devil

Conscience and grace, to the profoundest pit!

I dare damnation. To this point I stand,

That both the world, I give to negligence,

Let come what comes; only I'll be reveng'd

Most throughly for my father.

King: Who shall stay you?

Laertes: My will, not all the world!

And for my means, I'll husband them so well

They shall go far with little.

King: Good Laertes,

If you desire to know the certainty

Of your dear father's death, is't writ in your revenge

That swoopstake you will draw both friend and foe,

Winner and loser?

Laertes: None but his enemies.

King: Will you know them then?

Laertes: To his good friends thus wide I'll ope my arms

And, like the kind life-rend'ring pelican,

Repast them with my blood.

King: Why, now you speak

Like a good child and a true gentleman.

That I am guiltless of your father's death,

And am most sensibly in grief for it,

It shall as level to your judgment pierce

As day does to your eye.

[A noise within: 'Let her come in.']

Laertes: How now? What noise is that?

[Enter Ophelia.]

O heat, dry up my brains! Tears seven times salt

Burn out the sense and virtue of mine eye!

By heaven, thy madness shall be paid by weight

Till our scale turn the beam. O rose of May!

Dear maid, kind sister, sweet Ophelia!

O heavens! is't possible a young maid's wits

Should be as mortal as an old man's life?

Nature is fine in love, and where 'tis fine,

It sends some precious instance of itself

After the thing it loves.

Ophelia: (sings) *They bore him barefac'd on the bier*

 (Hey non nony, nony, hey nony)
And in his grave rain'd many a tear.
Fare you well, my dove!

Laertes: Hadst thou thy wits, and didst persuade revenge,

It could not move thus.

Ophelia: You must sing 'A-down a-down', and you call him 'a-down-a.' O, how the wheel becomes it! It is the false steward, that stole his master's daughter.

Laertes: This nothing's more than matter.

Ophelia: There's rosemary, that's for remembrance. Pray you, love,
Remember. And there is pansies, that's for thoughts.

Laertes: A document in madness! Thoughts and remembrance fitted.

Ophelia: There's fennel for you, and columbines. There's rue for you, and here's some for me. We may call it herb of grace o' Sundays. O, you must wear your rue with a difference! There's a daisy. I would give you some violets, but they wither'd all when my father died. They say he made a good end.

(Sings) *For bonny sweet Robin is all my joy.*

Laertes: Thought and affliction, passion, hell itself,

She turns to favour and to prettiness.

Ophelia: (sings) *And will he not come again?*

And will he not come again?

No, no, he is dead;

Go to thy deathbed;

He never will come again.

His beard was as white as snow,

All flaxen was his poll.

He is gone, he is gone,

And we cast away moan.

God 'a'mercy on his soul!

And of all Christian souls, I pray God. God b' wi', you.

[Exit.]

Laertes: Do you see this, O God?

King: Laertes, I must commune with your grief,

Or you deny me right. Go but apart,

Make choice of whom your wisest friends you

will,

And they shall hear and judge 'twixt you and me.

If by direct or by collateral hand

They find us touch'd, we will our kingdom give,

Our crown, our life, and all that we call ours,

To you in satisfaction; but if not,

Be you content to lend your patience to us,

And we shall jointly labour with your soul

To give it due content.

Laertes: Let this be so.

His means of death, his obscure funeral-

No trophy, sword, nor hatchment o'er his bones,

No noble rite nor formal ostentation,-

Cry to be heard, as 'twere from heaven to earth,

That I must call't in question.

King: So you shall;

And where th' offence is let the great axe fall.

I pray you go with me.

[Exeunt.]

Scene VI - Elsinore. Another room in the Castle.

[Enter Horatio and others.]

Horatio: What are they that would speak with me?

Servant: Seafaring men, sir. They say they have letters for you.

Horatio: Let them come in.

[Exit Attendant.]

I do not know from what part of the world
I should be greeted, if not from Lord Hamlet.

[Enter Sailors.]

Sailor: God bless you, sir.

Horatio: Let him bless thee too.

Sailor: 'A shall, sir, an't please him. There's a letter for you, sir,- it comes from th' ambassador that was bound for England, if your name be Horatio, as I am let to know it is.

Horatio: (reads the letter) *'Horatio, when thou shalt have overlook'd this, give these fellows some means to the King. They have letters for him. Ere we were two days old at sea, a pirate of very war-like appointment gave us chase. Finding ourselves too slow of sail, we put on a compelled valour, and in the grapple I boarded them. On the instant they got clear of our ship; so I alone became their prisoner. They have* *dealt with me like thieves of mercy; but they knew what they did: I am to do a good turn for them. Let the King have the letters I have sent, and repair thou to me with as much speed as thou wouldst fly death. I have words to speak in thine ear will make thee dumb; yet are they much too light for the bore of the matter. These good fellows will bring thee where I am. Rosencrantz and Guildenstern hold their course for England. Of them I have much to tell thee. Farewell.*

'He that thou knowest thine,
HAMLET.'

Come, I will give you way for these your letters,
And do't the speedier that you may direct me
To him from whom you brought them.
[Exeunt.]

Scene VII - Elsinore. Another room in the Castle.

[Enter King and Laertes.]

King: Now must your conscience my acquittance seal,
And you must put me in your heart for friend,

Sith you have heard, and with a knowing ear,

That he which hath your noble father slain

Pursued my life.

Laertes: It well appears. But tell me

Why you proceeded not against these feats

So crimeful and so capital in nature,

As by your safety, wisdom, all things else,

You mainly were stirr'd up.

King: O, for two special reasons,

Which may to you, perhaps, seein much

unsinew'd,

But yet to me they are strong. The Queen his

mother

Lives almost by his looks; and for myself,-

My virtue or my plague, be it either which,-

She's so conjunctive to my life and soul

That, as the star moves not but in his sphere,

I could not but by her. The other motive

Why to a public count I might not go

Is the great love the general gender bear him,

Who, dipping all his faults in their affection,

Would, like the spring that turneth wood to stone,

Convert his gives to graces; so that my arrows,

Too slightly timber'd for so loud a wind,

Would have reverted to my bow again,

And not where I had aim'd them.

Laertes: And so have I a noble father lost;

A sister driven into desp'rate terms,

Whose worth, if praises may go back again,

Stood challenger on mount of all the age

For her perfections. But my revenge will come.

King: Break not your sleeps for that. You must not think

That we are made of stuff so flat and dull

That we can let our beard be shook with danger,

And think it pastime. You shortly shall hear more.

I lov'd your father, and we love ourself,

And that, I hope, will teach you to imagine-

[Enter a Messenger with letters.]

How now? What news?

Messenger: Letters, my lord, from Hamlet.

This to your Majesty; this to the Queen.

King: From Hamlet? Who brought them?

Messenger: Sailors, my lord, they say; I saw them not.

They were given me by Claudio; he receiv'd them

Of him that brought them.

King: Laertes, you shall hear them.

Leave us.

[Exit Messenger.]

[Reads]*'High and Mighty,-You shall know I am set naked on your kingdom. To-morrow shall I beg leave to see your kingly eyes; when I shall (first asking your pardon thereunto) recount the occasion of my sudden and more strange return.*

      'HAMLET.'

What should this mean? Are all the rest come back?

Or is it some abuse, and no such thing?

Laertes: Know you the hand?

King: 'Tis Hamlet's character. 'Naked!'

And in a postscript here, he says 'alone.'

Can you advise me?

Laertes: I am lost in it, my lord. But let him come!

It warms the very sickness in my heart

That I shall live and tell him to his teeth,

'Thus didest thou.'

King: If it be so, Laertes

As how should it be so? how otherwise?

Will you be rul'd by me?

Laertes: Ay my lord,

So you will not o'errule me to a peace.

King: To thine own peace. If he be now return'd

As checking at his voyage, and that he means

No more to undertake it, I will work him

To exploit now ripe in my device,

Under the which he shall not choose but fall;

And for his death no wind

But even his mother shall uncharge the practice

And call it accident.

Laertes: My lord, I will be rul'd;

The rather, if you could devise it so

That I might be the organ.

King: It falls right.

You have been talk'd of since your travel much,

And that in Hamlet's hearing, for a quality

Wherein they say you shine, Your sun of parts

Did not together pluck such envy from him

As did that one; and that, in my regard,

Of the unworthiest siege.

Laertes: What part is that, my lord?

King: A very riband in the cap of youth-

Yet needfull too; for youth no less becomes

The light and careless livery that it wears

Thin settled age his sables and his weeds,

Importing health and graveness. Two months since

Here was a gentleman of Normandy.

I have seen myself, and serv'd against, the French,

And they can well on horseback; but this gallant

Had witchcraft in't. He grew unto his seat,

And to such wondrous doing brought his horse

As had he been incorps'd and demi-natur'd

With the brave beast. So far he topp'd my thought

That I, in forgery of shapes and tricks,

Come short of what he did.

Laertes: A Norman was't?

King: A Norman.

Laertes: Upon my life, Lamord.

King: The very same.

Laertes: I know him well. He is the broach indeed

And gem of all the nation.

King: He made confession of you;

And gave you such a masterly report

For art and exercise in your defence,

And for your rapier most especially,

That he cried out 'twould be a sight indeed

If one could match you. The scrimers of their

nation

He swore had neither motion, guard, nor eye,

If you oppos'd them. Sir, this report of his

Did Hamlet so envenom with his envy

That he could nothing do but wish and beg

Your sudden coming o'er to play with you.

Now, out of this-

Laertes: What out of this, my lord?

King: Laertes, was your father dear to you?

Or are you like the painting of a sorrow,

A face without a heart,'

Laertes: Why ask you this?

King: Not that I think you did not love your

father;

But that I know love is begun by time,

And that I see, in passages of proof,

Time qualifies the spark and fire of it.

There lives within the very flame of love

A kind of wick or snuff that will abate it;

And nothing is at a like goodness still;

For goodness, growing to a plurisy,

Dies in his own too-much. That we would do,

We should do when we would; for this 'would' changes,

And hath abatements and delays as many

As there are tongues, are hands, are accidents;

And then this 'should' is like a spendthrift sigh,

That hurts by easing. But to the quick o' th' ulcer!

Hamlet comes back. What would you undertake

To show yourself your father's son in deed

More than in words?

Laertes: To cut his throat i' th' church!

King: No place indeed should murder sanctuarize;

Revenge should have no bounds. But, good Laertes,

Will you do this? Keep close within your chamber.

Will return'd shall know you are come home.

We'll put on those shall praise your excellence

And set a double varnish on the fame

The Frenchman gave you; bring you in fine together

And wager on your heads. He, being remiss,

Most generous, and free from all contriving,

Will not peruse the foils; so that with ease,

Or with a little shuffling, you may choose

A sword unbated, and, in a pass of practice,

Requite him for your father.

Laertes: I will do't!

And for that purpose I'll anoint my sword.

I bought an unction of a mountebank,

So mortal that, but dip a knife in it,

Where it draws blood no cataplasm so rare,

Collected from all simples that have virtue

Under the moon, can save the thing from death

This is but scratch'd withal. I'll touch my point

With this contagion, that, if I gall him slightly,

It may be death.

King: Let's further think of this,

Weigh what convenience both of time and

means

May fit us to our shape. If this should fall,

And that our drift look through our bad

performance.

'Twere better not assay'd. Therefore this project

Should have a back or second, that might hold

If this did blast in proof. Soft! let me see.

We'll make a solemn wager on your cunnings-

I ha't!

When in your motion you are hot and dry-

As make your bouts more violent to that end-

And that he calls for drink, I'll have prepar'd him

A chalice for the nonce; whereon but sipping,

If he by chance escape your venom'd stuck,

Our purpose may hold there.- But stay, what noise,

[Enter Queen.]

How now, sweet queen?

Queen: One woe doth tread upon another's heel,

So fast they follow. Your sister's drown'd,

Laertes.

Laertes: Drown'd! O, where?

Queen: There is a willow grows aslant a brook,

That shows his hoar leaves in the glassy stream.

There with fantastic garlands did she come

Of crowflowers, nettles, daisies, and long purples,

That liberal shepherds give a grosser name,

But our cold maids do dead men's fingers call them.

There on the pendant boughs her coronet weeds

Clamb'ring to hang, an envious sliver broke,

When down her weedy trophies and herself

Fell in the weeping brook. Her clothes spread wide

And, mermaid-like, awhile they bore her up;

Which time she chanted snatches of old tunes,

As one incapable of her own distress,

Or like a creature native and indued

Unto that element; but long it could not be

Till that her garments, heavy with their drink,

Pull'd the poor wretch from her melodious lay

To muddy death.

Laertes: Alas, then she is drown'd?

Queen: Drown'd, drown'd.

Laertes: Too much of water hast thou, poor Ophelia,

And therefore I forbid my tears; but yet

It is our trick; nature her custom holds,

Let shame say what it will. When these are gone,

The woman will be out. Adieu, my lord.

I have a speech of fire, that fain would blaze

But that this folly douts it.

[Exit.]

King: Let's follow, Gertrude.

How much I had to do to calm his rage I

Now fear I this will give it start again;

Therefore let's follow.

[Exeunt.]

My Notes

ACT V

Scene I - Elsinore. A churchyard with a newly opened grave.

[Enter two Clowns, with spades and pickaxes.]

Clown: Is she to be buried in Christian burial when she wilfully seeks her own salvation?

Second Clown: I tell thee she is; therefore make her grave straight.
The crowner hath sate on her, and finds it Christian burial.

Clown: How can that be, unless she drown'd herself in her own defence?

Second Clown: Why, 'tis found so.

Clown: It must be *se offendendo*; it cannot be else. For here lies the point: if I drown myself wittingly, it argues an act; and an act hath three branches-it is to act, to do, and to perform; argal, she drown'd herself wittingly.

Second Clown: Nay, but hear you, goodman delver!

Clown: Give me leave. Here lies the water; good. Here stands the man; good. If the man go to this water and drown himself, it is, will he nill he, he goes- mark you that. But if the water come to him and drown him, he drowns not himself. Argal, he that is not guilty of his own death shortens not his own life.

Second Clown: But is this law?

Clown: Ay, marry, is't crowner's quest law.

Second Clown: Will you ha' the truth an't? If this had not been a gentlewoman, she should have been buried out o' Christian burial.

Clown: Why, there thou say'st! And the more pity that great folk should have count'nance in this world to drown or hang themselves more than their even-Christen. Come, my spade! There is no ancient gentlemen but gard'ners, ditchers, and grave-makers. They hold up Adam's profession.

Second Clown: Was he a gentleman?

Clown: 'A was the first that ever bore arms.

Second Clown: Why, he had none.

Clown: What, art a heathen? How dost thou understand the Scripture? The Scripture says Adam digg'd. Could he dig without arms? I'll put another question to thee. If thou answerest me not to the purpose, confess thyself-

Second Clown: Go to!

Clown: What is he that builds stronger than either the mason, the shipwright, or the carpenter?

Second Clown: The gallows-maker; for that frame outlives a thousand tenants.

Clown: I like thy wit well, in good faith. The gallows does well. But how does it well? It does well to those that do ill. Now, thou dost ill to say the gallows is built stronger than the church. Argal, the gallows may do well to thee. To't again, come!

Second Clown: Who builds stronger than a mason, a shipwright, or a carpenter?

Clown: Ay, tell me that, and unyoke.

Second Clown: Marry, now I can tell!

Clown: To't.

Second Clown: Mass, I cannot tell.

[Enter Hamlet and Horatio afar off.]

Clown: Cudgel thy brains no more about it, for your dull ass will not mend his pace with beating; and when you are ask'd this question next, say 'a grave-maker.' The houses he makes lasts till doomsday. Go, get thee to Yaughan; fetch me a stoup of liquor.

[Exit Second Clown.]

[Clown digs and sings.]

In youth when I did love, did love,

Methought it was very sweet;

To contract, o' the time for a my behove,

O, methought there a was nothing a meet.

Hamlet: Has this fellow no feeling of his business, that he sings at grave-making?

Horatio: Custom hath made it in him a property of easiness.

Hamlet: 'Tis e'en so. The hand of little employment hath the daintier sense.

Clown: (sings) *But age with his stealing steps*

Hath clawed me in his clutch,

And hath shipped me intil the land,

As if I had never been such.

[Throws up a skull.]

Hamlet: That skull had a tongue in it, and could sing once. How the knave jowls it to the ground, as if 'twere Cain's jawbone, that did the first murder! This might be the pate of a politician, which this ass now o'erreaches; one that would circumvent God, might it not?

Horatio: It might, my lord.

Hamlet: Or of a courtier, which could say 'Good morrow, sweet lord! How dost thou, good lord?' This might be my Lord Such-a-one, that prais'd my Lord Such-a-one's horse when he meant to beg it, might it not?

Horatio: Ay, my lord.

Hamlet: Why, e'en so! and now my Lady Worm's, chapless, and knock'd
about the mazzard with a sexton's spade. Here's fine revolution, and we had the trick to see't. Did these bones cost no more the breeding but to play at loggats with 'em? Mine ache to think on't.

Clown: (Sings) *A pickaxe and a spade, a spade,*
For and a shrouding sheet;
O, a Pit of clay for to be made
For such a guest is meet.

 [Throws up another skull].

Hamlet: There's another. Why may not that be the skull of a lawyer?
Where be his quiddits now, his quillets, his cases, his tenures, and his tricks? Why does he suffer this rude knave now to knock him about

the sconce with a dirty shovel, and will not tell him of his action of battery? Hum! This fellow might be in's time a great buyer of land, with his statutes, his recognizances, his fines, his double vouchers, his recoveries. Is this the fine of his fines, and the recovery of his recoveries, to have his fine pate full of fine dirt? Will his vouchers vouch him no more of his purchases, and double ones too, than the length and breadth of a pair of indentures? The very conveyances of his lands will scarcely lie in this box; and must th' inheritor himself have no more, ha?

Horatio: Not a jot more, my lord.

Hamlet: Is not parchment made of sheepskins?

Horatio: Ay, my lord, And of calveskins too.

Hamlet: They are sheep and calves which seek out assurance in that. I will speak to this fellow. Whose grave's this, sirrah?

Clown: Mine, sir.

[Sings] *O, a pit of clay for to be made*
For such a guest is meet.

Hamlet: I think it be thine indeed, for thou liest in't.

Clown: You lie out on't, sir, and therefore 'tis not

yours.

For my part, I do not lie in't, yet it is mine.

Hamlet: Thou dost lie in't, to be in't and say it is thine. 'Tis for the dead, not for the quick; therefore thou liest.

Clown: 'Tis a quick lie, sir; 'twill away again from me to you.

Hamlet: What man dost thou dig it for?

Clown: For no man, sir.

Hamlet: What woman then?

Clown: For none neither.

Hamlet: Who is to be buried in't?

Clown: One that was a woman, sir; but, rest her soul, she's dead.

Hamlet: How absolute the knave is! We must speak by the card, or equivocation will undo us. By the Lord, Horatio, this three years I have taken note of it, the age is grown so picked that the toe of the peasant comes so near the heel of the courtier he galls his kibe. How long hast thou been a grave-maker?

Clown: Of all the days i' th' year, I came to't that day that our last king Hamlet overcame Fortinbras.

Hamlet: How long is that since?

Clown: Cannot you tell that? Every fool can tell that. It was the very day that young Hamlet was born- he that is mad, and sent into England.

Hamlet: Ay, marry, why was be sent into England?

Clown: Why, because 'a was mad. 'A shall recover his wits there; or, if 'a do not, 'tis no great matter there.

Hamlet: Why?

Clown: 'Twill not he seen in him there. There the men are as mad as he.

Hamlet: How came he mad?

Clown: Very strangely, they say.

Hamlet: How strangely?

Clown: Faith, e'en with losing his wits.

Hamlet: Upon what ground?

Clown: Why, here in Denmark. I have been sexton here, man and boy thirty years.

Hamlet: How long will a man lie i' th' earth ere he rot?

Clown: Faith, if 'a be not rotten before 'a die (as we have many pocky corses nowadays that will scarce hold the laying in, I will last you some eight year or nine year. A tanner will last you nine year.

Hamlet: Why he more than another?

Clown: Why, sir, his hide is so tann'd with his trade that 'a will keep out water a great while; and your water is a sore decayer of your whoreson dead body. Here's a skull now. This skull hath lien you i' th' earth three-and-twenty years.

Hamlet: Whose was it?

Clown: A whoreson, mad fellow's it was. Whose do you think it was?

Hamlet: Nay, I know not.

Clown: A pestilence on him for a mad rogue! 'A pour'd a flagon of Rhenish on my head once. This same skull, sir, was Yorick's skull, the King's jester.

Hamlet: This?

Clown: E'en that.

Hamlet: Let me see. [Takes the skull.] Alas, poor Yorick! I knew him, Horatio. A fellow of infinite jest, of most excellent fancy. He hath borne me on his back a thousand tunes. And now how abhorred in my imagination it is! My gorge rises at it. Here hung those lips that I have kiss'd I know not how oft. Where be your gibes now? your gambols? your songs? your flashes of merriment that were wont to set the table on a roar? Not one now, to mock your own grinning? Quite chap- fall'n? Now get you to my lady's chamber, and tell her, let her paint an inch thick, to this favour she must come. Make her laugh at that. Prithee, Horatio, tell me one thing.

Horatio: What's that, my lord?

Hamlet: Dost thou think Alexander look'd o' this fashion i' th' earth?

Horatio: E'en so.

Hamlet: And smelt so? Pah!

[Puts down the skull.]

Horatio: E'en so, my lord.

Hamlet: To what base uses we may return, Horatio! Why may not imagination trace the noble dust of Alexander till he find it stopping a bunghole?

Horatio: 'Twere to consider too curiously, to consider so.

Hamlet: No, faith, not a jot; but to follow him thither with modesty enough, and likelihood to lead it; as thus: Alexander died, Alexander was buried, Alexander returneth into dust; the dust is earth; of earth we make loam; and why of that loam (whereto he was converted) might they not stop a beer barrel?

Imperious Caesar, dead and turn'd to clay,
Might stop a hole to keep the wind away.
O, that that earth which kept the world in awe
Should patch a wall t' expel the winter's flaw!

But soft! but soft! aside! Here comes the King-
[Enter priests with a coffin in funeral procession, King, Queen, Laertes, with Lords attendant.]
The Queen, the courtiers. Who is this they follow?
And with such maimed rites? This doth betoken
The corse they follow did with desp'rate hand
Fordo it own life. 'Twas of some estate.
Couch we awhile, and mark.
[Retires with Horatio.]

Laertes: What ceremony else?

Hamlet: That is Laertes,
A very noble youth. Mark.

Laertes: What ceremony else?

Priest: Her obsequies have been as far enlarg'd

As we have warranty. Her death was doubtful;

And, but that great command o'ersways the order,

She should in ground unsanctified have lodg'd

Till the last trumpet. For charitable prayers,

Shards, flints, and pebbles should be thrown on her.

Yet here she is allow'd her virgin crants,

Her maiden strewments, and the bringing home

Of bell and burial.

Laertes: Must there no more be done?

Priest: No more be done.

We should profane the service of the dead

To sing a requiem and such rest to her

As to peace-parted souls.

Laertes: Lay her i' th' earth;

And from her fair and unpolluted flesh

May violets spring! I tell thee, churlish priest,

A minist'ring angel shall my sister be

When thou liest howling.

Hamlet: What, the fair Ophelia?

Queen: Sweets to the sweet! Farewell.

[Scatters flowers.]

I hop'd thou shouldst have been my Hamlet's

wife;

I thought thy bride-bed to have deck'd, sweet maid,

And not have strew'd thy grave.

Laertes: O, treble woe

Fall ten times treble on that cursed head

Whose wicked deed thy most ingenious sense

Depriv'd thee of! Hold off the earth awhile,

Till I have caught her once more in mine arms.

[Leaps in the grave.]

Now pile your dust upon the quick and dead

Till of this flat a mountain you have made

T' o'ertop old Pelion or the skyish head

Of blue Olympus.

Hamlet: [comes forward] What is he whose grief

Bears such an emphasis? whose phrase of sorrow

Conjures the wand'ring stars, and makes them stand

Like wonder-wounded hearers? This is I,

Hamlet the Dane.

[Leaps in after Laertes.]

Laertes: The devil take thy soul!

[Grapples with him].

Hamlet: Thou pray'st not well.

I prithee take thy fingers from my throat;

For, though I am not splenitive and rash,

Yet have I in me something dangerous,

Which let thy wisdom fear. Hold off thy hand!

King: Pluck thein asunder.

Queen: Hamlet, Hamlet!

All: Gentlemen!

Horatio: Good my lord, be quiet.

[The Attendants part them, and they come out of the grave.]

Hamlet: Why, I will fight with him upon this theme

Until my eyelids will no longer wag.

Queen: O my son, what theme?

Hamlet: I lov'd Ophelia. Forty thousand brothers

Could not (with all their quantity of love)

Make up my sum. What wilt thou do for her?

King: O, he is mad, Laertes.

Queen: For love of God, forbear him!

Hamlet: 'Swounds, show me what thou't do.

Woo't weep? Woo't fight? Woo't fast? Woo't tear thyself?

Woo't drink up eisel? Eat a crocodile?

I'll do't. Dost thou come here to whine?

To outface me with leaping in her grave?

Be buried quick with her, and so will I.

And if thou prate of mountains, let them throw

Millions of acres on us, till our ground,

Singeing his pate against the burning zone,

Make Ossa like a wart! Nay, an thou'lt mouth,

I'll rant as well as thou.

Queen: This is mere madness;

And thus a while the fit will work on him.

Anon, as patient as the female dove

When that her golden couplets are disclos'd,

His silence will sit drooping.

Hamlet: Hear you, sir!

What is the reason that you use me thus?

I lov'd you ever. But it is no matter.

Let Hercules himself do what he may,

The cat will mew, and dog will have his day.

[Exit.]

King: I pray thee, good Horatio, wait upon him.

[Exit Horatio.]

[To Laertes] Strengthen your patience in our last

night's speech.

We'll put the matter to the present push.

Good Gertrude, set some watch over your son.

This grave shall have a living monument.

An hour of quiet shortly shall we see;

Till then in patience our proceeding be.

[Exeunt.]

Scene II - Elsinore. A hall in the Castle.

[Enter Hamlet and Horatio.]

Hamlet: So much for this, sir; now shall you see the other.

You do remember all the circumstance?

Horatio: Remember it, my lord!

Hamlet: Sir, in my heart there was a kind of fighting

That would not let me sleep. Methought I lay

Worse than the mutinies in the bilboes. Rashly-

And prais'd be rashness for it; let us know,

Our indiscretion sometime serves us well

When our deep plots do pall; and that should learn us

There's a divinity that shapes our ends,

Rough-hew them how we will-

Horatio: That is most certain.

Hamlet: Up from my cabin,

My sea-gown scarf'd about me, in the dark

Grop'd I to find out them; had my desire,

Finger'd their packet, and in fine withdrew

To mine own room again; making so bold

(My fears forgetting manners) to unseal

Their grand commission; where I found, Horatio

(O royal knavery!), an exact command,

Larded with many several sorts of reasons,

Importing Denmark's health, and England's too,

With, hoo! such bugs and goblins in my life-

That, on the supervise, no leisure bated,

No, not to stay the finding of the axe,

My head should be struck off.

Horatio: Is't possible?

Hamlet: Here's the commission; read it at more

leisure.

But wilt thou bear me how I did proceed?

Horatio: I beseech you.

Hamlet: Being thus benetted round with villanies,

Or I could make a prologue to my brains,

They had begun the play. I sat me down;

Devis'd a new commission; wrote it fair.

I once did hold it, as our statists do,

A baseness to write fair, and labour'd much

How to forget that learning; but, sir, now

It did me yeoman's service. Wilt thou know

Th' effect of what I wrote?

Horatio: Ay, good my lord.

Hamlet: An earnest conjuration from the King,

As England was his faithful tributary,

As love between them like the palm might

flourish,

As peace should still her wheaten garland wear

And stand a comma 'tween their amities,

And many such-like as's of great charge,

That, on the view and knowing of these contents,

Without debatement further, more or less,

He should the bearers put to sudden death,

Not shriving time allow'd.

Horatio: How was this seal'd?

Hamlet: Why, even in that was heaven ordinant.

I had my father's signet in my purse,

which was the model of that Danish seal;

Folded the writ up in the form of th' other,

Subscrib'd it, gave't th' impression, plac'd it

safely,

The changeling never known. Now, the next day

Was our sea-fight; and what to this was sequent
Thou know'st already.

Horatio: So Guildenstern and Rosencrantz go to't.

Hamlet: Why, man, they did make love to this employment!
They are not near my conscience; their defeat
Does by their own insinuation grow.
'Tis dangerous when the baser nature comes
Between the pass and fell incensed points
Of mighty opposites.

Horatio: Why, what a king is this!

Hamlet: Does it not, thinks't thee, stand me now upon-
He that hath kill'd my king, and whor'd my mother;
Popp'd in between th' election and my hopes;
Thrown out his angle for my Proper life,
And with such coz'nage- is't not perfect conscience
To quit him with this arm? And is't not to be damn'd
To let this canker of our nature come
In further evil?

Horatio: It must be shortly known to him from England

What is the issue of the business there.

Hamlet: It will be short; the interim is mine,

And a man's life is no more than to say 'one'.

But I am very sorry, good Horatio,

That to Laertes I forgot myself,

For by the image of my cause I see

The portraiture of his. I'll court his favours.

But sure the bravery of his grief did put me

Into a tow'ring passion.

Horatio: Peace! Who comes here?

[Enter young Osric, a courtier.]

Osric: Your lordship is right welcome back to Denmark.

Hamlet: I humbly thank you, sir. [Aside to Horatio] Dost know this waterfly?

Horatio: [aside to Hamlet] No, my good lord.

Hamlet: [aside to Horatio] Thy state is the more gracious; for 'tis a vice to know him. He hath much land, and fertile. Let a beast be lord of beasts, and his crib shall stand at the king's mess. 'Tis a chough; but, as I say, spacious in the possession of dirt.

Osric: Sweet lord, if your lordship were at leisure, I should impart a thing to you from his Majesty.

Hamlet: I will receive it, sir, with all diligence of spirit. Put your bonnet to his right use. 'Tis for the head.

Osric: I thank your lordship, it is very hot.

Hamlet: No, believe me, 'tis very cold; the wind is northerly.

Osric: It is indifferent cold, my lord, indeed.

Hamlet: But yet methinks it is very sultry and hot for my complexion.

Osric: Exceedingly, my lord; it is very sultry, as 'twere- I cannot tell how. But, my lord, his Majesty bade me signify to you that he has laid a great wager on your head. Sir, this is the matter-

Hamlet: I beseech you remember.

[Hamlet moves him to put on his hat.]

Osric: Nay, good my lord; for mine ease, in good faith. Sir, here is newly come to court Laertes; believe me, an absolute gentleman, full of most excellent differences, of very soft society and great showing. Indeed, to speak feelingly of him, he is the card or calendar of gentry; for you shall find in him the continent of what part a gentleman would see.

Hamlet: Sir, his definement suffers no perdition in you; though, I know, to divide him inventorially would dozy th' arithmetic of memory, and yet but yaw neither in respect of his quick sail. But, in the verity of extolment, I take him to be a soul of great article, and his infusion of such dearth and rareness as, to make true diction of him, his semblable is his mirror, and who else would trace him, his umbrage, nothing more.

Osric: Your lordship speaks most infallibly of him.

Hamlet: The concernancy, sir? Why do we wrap the gentleman in our more rawer breath.

Osric: Sir?

Horatio: [aside to Hamlet] Is't not possible to understand in another tongue? You will do't, sir, really.

Hamlet: What imports the nomination of this gentleman

Osric: Of Laertes?

Horatio: [aside] His purse is empty already. All's golden words are spent.

Hamlet: Of him, sir.

Osric: I know you are not ignorant-

Hamlet: I would you did, sir; yet, in faith, if you did, it would not much approve me. Well, sir?

Osric: You are not ignorant of what excellence Laertes is-

Hamlet: I dare not confess that, lest I should compare with him in excellence; but to know a man well were to know himself.

Osric: I mean, sir, for his weapon; but in the imputation laid on him by them, in his meed he's unfellowed.

Hamlet: What's his weapon?

Osric: Rapier and dagger.

Hamlet: That's two of his weapons- but well.

Osric: The King, sir, hath wager'd with him six Barbary horses; against the which he has impon'd, as I take it, six French rapiers and poniards, with their assigns, as girdle, hangers, and so. Three of the carriages, in faith, are very dear to fancy, very responsive to the hilts, most delicate carriages, and of very liberal conceit.

Hamlet: What call you the carriages?

Horatio: [aside to Hamlet] I knew you must be

edified by the margent ere you had done.

Osric: The carriages, sir, are the hangers.

Hamlet: The phrase would be more germane to the matter if we could carry cannon by our sides. I would it might be hangers till then. But on! Six Barbary horses against six French swords, their assigns, and three liberal-conceited carriages: that's the French bet against the Danish. Why is this all impon'd, as you call it?

Osric: The King, sir, hath laid that, in a dozen passes between yourself and him, he shall not exceed you three hits; he hath laid on twelve for nine, and it would come to immediate trial if your lordship would vouchsafe the answer.

Hamlet: How if I answer no?

Osric: I mean, my lord, the opposition of your person in trial.

Hamlet: Sir, I will walk here in the hall. If it please his Majesty, it is the breathing time of day with me. Let the foils be brought, the gentleman willing, and the King hold his purpose, I will win for him if I can; if not, I will gain nothing but my shame and the odd hits.

Osric: Shall I redeliver you e'en so?

Hamlet: To this effect, sir, after what flourish your nature will.

Osric: I commend my duty to your lordship.

Hamlet: Yours, yours. [Exit Osric.] He does well to commend it himself; there are no tongues else for's turn.

Horatio: This lapwing runs away with the shell on his head.

Hamlet: He did comply with his dug before he suck'd it. Thus has he, and many more of the same bevy that I know the drossy age dotes on, only got the tune of the time and outward habit of encounter; a kind of yesty collection, which carries them through and through the most fann'd and winnowed opinions; and do but blow them to their trial-the bubbles are out.

[Enter a Lord.]

Lord: My lord, his Majesty commended him to you by young Osric, who brings back to him, that you attend him in the hall. He sends to know if your pleasure hold to play with Laertes, or that you will take longer time.

Hamlet: I am constant to my purposes; they follow the King's pleasure.

If his fitness speaks, mine is ready; now or whensoever, provided

I be so able as now.

Lord: The King and Queen and all are coming down.

Hamlet: In happy time.

Lord: The Queen desires you to use some gentle entertainment to Laertes before you fall to play.

Hamlet: She well instructs me.

[Exit Lord.]

Horatio: You will lose this wager, my lord.

Hamlet: I do not think so. Since he went into France I have been in continual practice. I shall win at the odds. But thou wouldst not think how ill all's here about my heart. But it is no matter.

Horatio: Nay, good my lord -

Hamlet: It is but foolery; but it is such a kind of gain-giving as would perhaps trouble a woman.

Horatio: If your mind dislike anything, obey it. I will forestall their repair hither and say you are not fit.

Hamlet: Not a whit, we defy augury; there's a special providence in the fall of a sparrow. If it be now, 'tis not to come', if it be not to come, it will be now; if it be not now, yet it will come: the readiness is all. Since no man knows aught of what he leaves, what is't to leave betimes? Let be.

[Enter King, Queen, Laertes, Osric, and Lords, with other Attendants with foils and gauntlets.]

[A table and flagons of wine on it.]

King: Come, Hamlet, come, and take this hand from me.

[The King puts Laertes' hand into Hamlet's.]

Hamlet: [To Laertes] Give me your pardon, sir. I have done you wrong;

But pardon't, as you are a gentleman.

This presence knows,

And you must needs have heard, how I am punish'd

With sore distraction. What I have done

That might your nature, honour, and exception

Roughly awake, I here proclaim was madness.

Was't Hamlet wrong'd Laertes? Never Hamlet.

If Hamlet from himself be taken away,

And when he's not himself does wrong Laertes,

Then Hamlet does it not, Hamlet denies it.

Who does it, then? His madness. If't be so,

Hamlet is of the faction that is wrong'd;

His madness is poor Hamlet's enemy.

Sir, in this audience,

Let my disclaiming from a purpos'd evil

Free me so far in your most generous thoughts

That I have shot my arrow o'er the house

And hurt my brother.

Laertes: I am satisfied in nature,

Whose motive in this case should stir me most

To my revenge. But in my terms of honour

I stand aloof, and will no reconcilement

Till by some elder masters of known honour

I have a voice and precedent of peace

To keep my name ungor'd. But till that time

I do receive your offer'd love like love,

And will not wrong it.

Hamlet: I embrace it freely,

And will this brother's wager frankly play.

Give us the foils. Come on.

Laertes: Come, one for me.

Hamlet: I'll be your foil, Laertes. In mine ignorance

Your skill shall, like a star i' th' darkest night,

Stick fiery off indeed.

Laertes: You mock me, sir.

Hamlet: No, by this bad.

King: Give them the foils, young Osric. Cousin Hamlet,

You know the wager?

Hamlet: Very well, my lord.

Your Grace has laid the odds o' th' weaker side.

King: I do not fear it, I have seen you both;

But since he is better'd, we have therefore odds.

Laertes: This is too heavy; let me see another.

Hamlet: This likes me well. These foils have all a length?

[Prepare to play.]

Osric: Ay, my good lord.

King: Set me the stoups of wine upon that table.

If Hamlet give the first or second hit,

Or quit in answer of the third exchange,

Let all the battlements their ordnance fire;

The King shall drink to Hamlet's better breath,

And in the cup an union shall he throw

Richer than that which four successive kings

In Denmark's crown have worn. Give me the cups;

And let the kettle to the trumpet speak,

The trumpet to the cannoneer without,

The cannons to the heavens, the heaven to earth,

'Now the King drinks to Hamlet.' Come, begin.

And you the judges, bear a wary eye.

Hamlet: Come on, sir.

Laertes: Come, my lord.

[They play.]

Hamlet: One.

Laertes: No.

Hamlet: Judgment!

Osric: A hit, a very palpable hit.

Laertes: Well, again!

King: Stay, give me drink. Hamlet, this pearl is thine;

Here's to thy health.

[Drum; trumpets sound; a piece goes off within.]

Give him the cup.

Hamlet: I'll play this bout first; set it by awhile.

Come. (They play.) Another hit. What say you?

Laertes: A touch, a touch; I do confess't.

King: Our son shall win.

Queen: He's fat, and scant of breath.

Here, Hamlet, take my napkin, rub thy brows.

The Queen carouses to thy fortune, Hamlet.

Hamlet: Good madam!

King: Gertrude, do not drink.

Queen: I will, my lord; I pray you pardon me.

[Drinks.]

King: [aside] It is the poison'd cup; it is too late.

Hamlet: I dare not drink yet, madam; by-and-by.

Queen: Come, let me wipe thy face.

Laertes: My lord, I'll hit him now.

King: I do not think't.

Laertes: [aside] And yet it is almost against my conscience.

Hamlet: Come for the third, Laertes! You but dally.

pray you pass with your best violence;

I am afeard you make a wanton of me.

Laertes: Say you so? Come on.

[Play.]

Osric: Nothing neither way.

Laertes: Have at you now!

[Laertes wounds Hamlet; then in scuffling, they change rapiers, and Hamlet wounds Laertes].

King: Part them! They are incens'd.

Hamlet: Nay come! again!

[The Queen falls.]

Osric: Look to the Queen there, ho!

Horatio: They bleed on both sides. How is it, my lord?

Osric: How is't, Laertes?

Laertes: Why, as a woodcock to mine own springe, Osric.

I am justly kill'd with mine own treachery.

Hamlet: How does the Queen?

King: She sounds to see them bleed.

Queen: No, no! the drink, the drink! O my dear Hamlet!

The drink, the drink! I am poison'd.

[Dies.]

Hamlet: O villany! Ho! let the door be lock'd.

Treachery! Seek it out.

[Laertes falls.]

Laertes: It is here, Hamlet. Hamlet, thou art slain;

No medicine in the world can do thee good.

In thee there is not half an hour of life.

The treacherous instrument is in thy hand,

Unbated and envenom'd. The foul practice

Hath turn'd itself on me. Lo, here I lie,

Never to rise again. Thy mother's poison'd.

I can no more. The King, the King's to blame.

Hamlet: The point envenom'd too?

Then, venom, to thy work.

[Stabs the King.]

All: Treason! treason!

King: O, yet defend me, friends! I am but hurt.

Hamlet: Here, thou incestuous, murd'rous,

damned Dane,

Drink off this potion! Is thy union here?

Follow my mother.

[King dies.]

Laertes: He is justly serv'd.

It is a poison temper'd by himself.

Exchange forgiveness with me, noble Hamlet.

Mine and my father's death come not upon thee,

Nor thine on me!

[Dies.]

Hamlet: Heaven make thee free of it! I follow

thee.

I am dead, Horatio. Wretched queen, adieu!

You that look pale and tremble at this chance,

That are but mutes or audience to this act,

Had I but time (as this fell sergeant, Death,

Is strict in his arrest) O, I could tell you-

But let it be. Horatio, I am dead;

Thou liv'st; report me and my cause aright

To the unsatisfied.

Horatio: Never believe it.

I am more an antique Roman than a Dane.

Here's yet some liquor left.

Hamlet: As th'art a man,

Give me the cup. Let go! By heaven, I'll ha't.

O good Horatio, what a wounded name

(Things standing thus unknown) shall live behind

me!

If thou didst ever hold me in thy heart,

Absent thee from felicity awhile,

And in this harsh world draw thy breath in pain,

To tell my story.

[March afar off, and shot within.]

What warlike noise is this?

Osric: Young Fortinbras, with conquest come

from Poland,

To the ambassadors of England gives

This warlike volley.

Hamlet: O, I die, Horatio!

The potent poison quite o'ercrows my spirit.

I cannot live to hear the news from England,

But I do prophesy th' election lights

On Fortinbras. He has my dying voice.

So tell him, with th' occurrents, more and less,

Which have solicited- the rest is silence.

[Dies.]

Horatio: Now cracks a noble heart. Good night, sweet prince,

And flights of angels sing thee to thy rest!

[March within.]

Why does the drum come hither?

[Enter Fortinbras, English Ambassadors, and Attendants.]

Fortinbras: Where is this sight?

Horatio: What is it you will see?

If aught of woe or wonder, cease your search.

Fortinbras: This quarry cries on havoc. O proud Death,

What feast is toward in thine eternal cell

That thou so many princes at a shot

So bloodily hast struck.

Ambassador: The sight is dismal;

And our affairs from England come too late.

The ears are senseless that should give us bearing

To tell him his commandment is fulfill'd

That Rosencrantz and Guildenstern are dead.

Where should we have our thanks?

Horatio: Not from his mouth,

Had it th' ability of life to thank you.

He never gave commandment for their death.

But since, so jump upon this bloody question,

You from the Polack wars, and you from England,

Are here arriv'd, give order that these bodies

High on a stage be placed to the view;

And let me speak to the yet unknowing world

How these things came about. So shall you hear

Of carnal, bloody and unnatural acts;

Of accidental judgments, casual slaughters;

Of deaths put on by cunning and forc'd cause;

And, in this upshot, purposes mistook

Fall'n on th' inventors' heads. All this can I

Truly deliver.

Fortinbras: Let us haste to hear it,

And call the noblest to the audience.

For me, with sorrow I embrace my fortune.

I have some rights of memory in this kingdom

Which now, to claim my vantage doth invite me.

Horatio: Of that I shall have also cause to speak,

And from his mouth whose voice will draw on more.

But let this same be presently perform'd,

Even while men's minds are wild, lest more mischance

On plots and errors happen.

Fortinbras: Let four captains

Bear Hamlet like a soldier to the stage;

For he was likely, had he been put on,

To have prov'd most royally; and for his passage

The soldiers' music and the rites of war

Speak loudly for him.

Take up the bodies. Such a sight as this

Becomes the field but here shows much amiss.

Go, bid the soldiers shoot.

[Soldiers bear away the bodies; after the which a peal of ordnance are shot off.]

My Notes

Glossary of Literary Terms

Alliteration: The occurrence of identical sounds, most often at the beginning of words e.g. "From forth the fatal loins of these two foes"

Allusion: An indirect reference to something

Anaphora: Repetition of the same word or phrase at the beginning of consecutive lines

Antagonist: The **protagonist**'s main adversary.

Antithesis: A person or thing that is the opposite of something else

Aside: A character's remark that is only meant to be heard by the audience but unheard by other characters in the play

Assonance: The resemblance of sounds between vowels of words in close proximity to one another

Blank verse: **Poetry** written with a regular **metre** but unrhymed, almost always in **iambic pentameter**

Climax: The dramatic end to the main **plot**. This is usually followed by **falling action**

Couplet: Two successive rhyming lines

Dramatic monologue: A poem in the form of a speech of an individual character

Euphemism: A gentle way of expressing something unpleasant

Falling Action: The section of a story following the **climax** but before the very end of the story

Foil: A character providing a contrast with another

Foot: A combination of stressed and unstressed syllables

Heroic couplet: a pair of rhyming **iambic pentameters**

Hyperbole: Exaggerated statements not meant to be taken literally

Iambic pentameter: A line of verse with five metrical feet, each consisting of one unstressed syllable followed by one stressed syllable

Imagery: A visually descriptive use of language

Internal rhyme: A rhyme involving a word in the middle of a line

Metaphor: A figure of speech that applies words to describe something in a non-literal way (e.g. *coal black eyes*). Metaphors do not use the words "like" or "as". If these words are used it is a **simile** (e.g. *eyes as black as coal*, or *eyes like black coal*).

Metre: The basic rhythmic structure of a verse or lines in a verse

Motif: An image or idea that runs through a play or novel

Onomatopoeia: A word that resembles the sound it is describing e.g. cuckoo, woof, burp, etc

Oxymoron: A figure of speech containing contradictory words, e.g. deafening silence

Paradox: A statement that contradicts itself e.g "This sentence is not true"

Personification: Attributing human characteristics to inanimate things

Plot: The events that make up the main part of a story

Poetry: Rhymed or rhythmic text

Pronoun: Referring to a person or thing, e.g. I, you, she, this, that

Prose: Written or spoken language without rhyme or rhythm

Protagonist: The lead character

Quatrain: A **stanza** of four lines

Refrain: A word or series of words repeated at intervals within a poem

Simile: A figure of speech containing "as" or "like" to describe something in a non-literal way (e.g. eyes like black coal). If the words "like" or "as" are not used then it is a **metaphor** (e.g. coal black eyes).

Soliloquy: A speech spoken by a character when alone, revealing their innermost thoughts

Sonnet: A fourteen-line poem.

Stanza: A group of poetic lines resembling paragraphs in **prose**

Sub-plot: A plot separate to the main **plot**

Syntax: The arrangement of words and phrases within a sentence

Tragic Hero: Generally the **protagonist** whose flaws or mistakes lead to their downfall

Hamlet Glossary

Antic – Mad

Apoplex'd – Paralysed

Argal – Therefore

Arras – A tapestry

Augury – An omen, or a prediction or foreshadowing of the future

Beaver – Visor, or a part of a helmet that covers the face

Bilboes – Stocks used aboard ships

Bisson rheum – Blinding tears

Bodkin – A dagger

Cap-a-pe – Head to foot

Carbuncle – A precious stone

Cataplasm – Poultice, bandages

Cautel – Deceit

Cellarage – Space below the stage accessible by trapdoor

Cerement – A pall or burial garment in which a corpse is placed

Cess – Cessation or stopping

Chopine – A shoe with a cork heel

Cicatrice – Scar

Climatures – Regions

Co-mart – Joint bargain

Countenance – Favour or support

Dansker – A Dane

Declension – Deterioration

Down-gyved – Hanging down to the ankle

Drabbing – Visiting prostitutes

Ducat – A gold coin

Dup – To open

Eisel – Vinegar

Espials – Spies

Excrements – Something that grows from the human body

Eyas – Fledgling hawk

Eyrie – A nest

Fardel – Bundle or pack

Gib – A tomcat; also a term of reproach

Good-mother – Stepmother

Green – Naive, inexperienced

Groundlings – Theatregoers who paid the smallest entry fee and had to stand to watch the show

Gules – Red, according to heraldic terminology

Gulf – Whirlpool

Harrow – Fills with worry or fear

Hic et ubique – Here and everywhere

Hoodman-blind – Blindman's buff

Hugger-mugger – Secrecy

Hymen – God of marriage

Hyperion – God of the sun

Hyrcanian beast – Tiger

Illume – To illuminate, make light

Importunity – Urgent solicitation

Lard – To garnish

Lethe – The river of forgetfulness in Hades

Limed – Caught

Matin – Dawn

Mazzard – Head

Miching mallecho – A stealthy crime

Milch – Milky

Mobled – Muffled

Moiety – Portion

Mote – A speck of dust

Mounteback – Fraudster

Nemean lion – Beast slain by Hercules

Nonce – Occasion

O'ercrow – Triumph over

Orisons – Prayers

Paddock – A toad

Parley – Debate

Perpend – Consider

Petar – Bomb

Porpentine – Porcupine

Posset – Curdle

Quietus – Discharge

Rivals – Partners

Robustious – Boisterous

Rood – Christ's cross

Roscius – A famous Roman actor

Rub – Obstacle

Scullion – Kitchen servant

Shent – Reproved

Splenative – Quick-tempered

Springes – Snares

Statist – A statesman

Stoup – A drinking vessel

Suppliance – Entertaining diversion

Tellus – The Roman goddess of the earth

Termagent – An angry deity often represented in medieval mystery plays

Tetter – An eruption on the skin

Unaneled – Unanointed

Unhouseled – Not cleansed by sacrament

Unsifted – Inexperienced

Ventages – Finger holes in a wind instrument

Videlicet – In other words

Wassail – Revelry, carousing
Wormwood – A bitter plant

For more on our large print, dyslexia-friendly, and annotation-friendly books, as well as our bulk discounts for schools visit:

firestonebooks.com

Printed in Great Britain
by Amazon